PRAISE FOR *RESILIENCE RECIPES*

This book is an immensely valuable resource for anyone wanting to take control of their wellbeing. Fleur Heazlewood uses her 20 years of experience and draws together some of the latest scientific evidence to provide a collection of self-guided strategies to help people to build their resilience. The book is practical and short, yet full of carefully designed activities that are both insightful and enjoyable to complete. It would make an excellent companion resource for workplace training programs aimed to enhance employee wellbeing.
Gavin Slemp, Senior Lecturer, Centre for the Science of Wellbeing, University of Melbourne

Resilience Recipes is the first book I have read that allows me to tailor my path based on what's important to me. It is like having your own mentor guiding you to transform on your terms. This book proves that with the right wisdom and guidance we can all become master chefs of our own wellbeing.
Barry Hemsley, Leader, Australian Public Service (APS)

Resilience Recipes is important because, frankly, wellness is exhausting! I love the simplicity of the tools and the connectivity with Fleur's personal experiences and vulnerability.

I have had the pleasure of working with Fleur for over ten years and have found her to be my go-to for advice and coaching and a great source of energy. Fleur's passion for helping and challenging people to truly be their version of the best they can be shines brightly through this book.
Kim Cheney, Head of HR – fintech, wine and fast-moving consumer goods

In this post-pandemic era, when wellbeing is top of mind for so many of us, this is a much-needed book that could not be more timely.

Fleur has worked across a multitude of organisations and improves the wellbeing of everyone she encounters. She leaves a lasting positive impact. This collective wisdom has culminated in this book, which brings years of work and learning into an easy to reread, practical guide.

Resilience Recipes is a must-read for anyone in need of practical advice on where to start their wellbeing journey.
Colleen O'Connor, Head of HR, Goodman Fielder

After the challenges we have all faced, wellbeing – both physical and mental – should be top of everyone's agenda. Fleur's book is a really great mix of philosophies, simple frameworks and practical tools to assist anyone leading teams through periods of change and uncertainty.

The strength of the message is the practical application and examples shared through her lived experience with many businesses. Fleur continuously rolls her sleeves up to support teams as they work through the challenges they face. It is this hands-on and delivered support that makes Fleur such a strong thought leader in this area.
Gavan McKenna, Group President at ITW Construction Products Asia Pacific

Resilience is the critical ingredient to living a balanced and rewarding life. Fleur is the right person to bring this book to the world as she has powerful lived experience to share.

I found this book a pleasure to read. It had a good measure of case studies and theories with practical tips for building resilience. You will finish the book with a sense of lightness and new insights into wellbeing that will work.
Simone Allan, Founder, Women's Resilience Centre

Fabulous! So easy to read, with simple and practical exercises that don't make you feel like you're taking on the world or trying to implement such large-scale transformations. We need a common-sense book like this that helps us to take back control and prioritise our own health and wellbeing.
Tammy Love, APS leadership program

From training rooms to text, Fleur's delivery is on point and memorable, and merges real-life experience with tools that embed learnings.

Thinking about my resilience and wellbeing journey metaphorically, I was busy, stressed and my axe was blunt – I could only cut down 100 trees a day. However, I could cut down 200 trees a day with a sharp axe; the issue was, I didn't have the time to sharpen it. Fleur's learnings sharpened my axe.
Jon Hill, General Manager, MCM Frame & Truss

RESILIENCE RECIPES

RESILIENCE

Making space for wellbeing that works

RECIPES

Fleur Heazlewood

This book is dedicated to you.

*In acknowledgement of the unique human being that you are.
For there is no-one else on this earth exactly like you –
that has your gifts, talents, perspectives and strengths.*

You deserve happiness, wellbeing and every success.

First published in 2022 by Major Street Publishing Pty Ltd
E: info@majorstreet.com.au W: majorstreet.com.au M: +61 421 707 983

NATIONAL LIBRARY OF AUSTRALIA

A catalogue record for this book is available from the National Library of Australia

Printed book ISBN: 978-1-922611-22-2
Ebook ISBN: 978-1-922611-23-9

Cover design by Tess McCabe
Internal design by Production Works
Printed in Australia by Ovato, an Accredited ISO AS/NZS 14001:2004 Environmental Management System Printer.

10 9 8 7 6 5 4 3 2 1

CONTENTS

ABOUT THE AUTHOR

With over 20 years' corporate leadership experience, Fleur has led many successful organisational turnarounds and culture transformations. She understands first-hand the challenges of change, uncertainty, staff stress and top talent burnout.

Fleur is known for building positive performing cultures that deliver both employee wellbeing and commercial results. She partners with CEOs, HR and leaders to create healthy, resilient and productive workplaces. Clients value her accessibility, practicality and skilled use of lessons that work in real life.

Fleur has trained and mentored over 1000 people in positive leadership, mental health mastery and future-fit resilience building. She consistently receives ratings of 90% and above for engagement and effectiveness of learning.

Fleur works with many of Australia's high-profile organisations, including the Department of Veterans' Affairs, Woolworths, BIG W, GenesisCare, ITW Construction, the Mental Health Commission of New South Wales and the Country Fire Authority.

Fleur's experience is backed by extensive qualifications, which include a Master of Coaching Psychology from the University of Sydney, a Bachelor of Commerce from the University of

Melbourne, a Company Directors Certificate from the Australian Institute of Company Directors and a Mental Health First Aid Instructor Certificate. Fleur also lectures in Organisational Culture and Wellbeing at the University of Melbourne and is a 500-hour certified yoga teacher.

ACKNOWLEDGEMENTS

When I was little, I enjoyed writing stories, creating pictures and making homemade books. As an adult, I found the process of pinning down all the fabulous ideas whizzing around in my head and getting them down on paper torturous!

Resilience Recipes would not have come to life without the support and cheerleading from my amazing team. It is connection rather than content that creates the magic.

Much love and appreciation to:

- Justin, for your love, unwavering patience and encouragement, and for having my back.
- Mum and Dad, for an upbringing and belief that anything is possible if you work for it.
- Chloe and Stephen, for bringing both scaffolding and support to my book and business growth.
- My clients and the amazing people that I have had the privilege to meet through my coaching, mentoring and training programs. Without you this journey of bringing wellbeing to our workplaces wouldn't have happened. Without you on board, this book wouldn't have happened, and I wouldn't know whether any of this actually… worked!

- The Anahata yoga community, who helped me find the space, slow the pace, reconnect with love and manifest a calmer way of living. Gratitude especially to Peter, Brigitte, Nina, Karo, Herbie, Dave and James.
- Matt, Lisa and the TLBS community, for a safe yet stretchy space to grow, connect and learn. Everyone needs a tribe where they are seen, heard and belong. This includes my Fab 5 of Ishan, Bernard, Anthony and Andrew who lovingly staged wellbeing interventions during the times I was stretching myself a bit too thin.

A huge thank you to:

- Colleen, Gavan, Barry, Tammy, Kim, Simone, Jon and Gavin, for sharing and championing the importance of wellbeing for all with me. Much more than colleagues to me, your kind words of endorsement mean a lot.
- The extraordinary Kelly Irving, who gave me the writing structure, coaching and gentle butt-kicking I needed to bring this book to fruition.
- The fabulous team at Major Street Publishing, who took my raw draft and elevated it to a first book that I am proud to share with the world.

INTRODUCTION

Life is a glorious work in progress – like one of Monet's beautiful, shining, inspiring waterlily masterpieces that packs a visual, emotional punch and then leaves you wondering what is just beyond the horizon.

However, many of us lose sight of the wonder of our life as we focus on the flaws that are stopping us from having more, progressing further or being better.

The way we live today is very different to the way generations before us lived.

I am sure you can relate to some of the following…

It is mid-afternoon and you are stressing at work, because after a day of interruptions you are behind on the day's deadlines. You eat takeaway lunch at your desk in a bid to catch up.

You are writing a report for your manager and answering a phone call from a colleague who has been chasing you for two days when you see a text pop up from your partner with a reminder that it is your turn to pick up the kids from school. You check the time and realise you are underprepared and now late for your next meeting.

You find it difficult to concentrate or contribute in the meeting, despite it being about something you care about and that will impact your workload, because your mind is consumed with your overflowing to-do list and rising stress levels.

You race out of the meeting, hastily scribble yourself some Post-it-Note reminders and then run out the door. You cut it fine to pick up your kids from school and chauffeur them to sport, play dates and a fitting for new sneakers before the shops close. All the while, you try to fit work phone calls and emails into the cracks.

Back at home, you are greeted by your partner, who wants to share their day's challenges with you. You do your best to engage while also helping the kids with homework, putting on a load of washing and organising dinner.

The house finally quietens, your partner is cleaning up the kitchen and you flop down on the couch to switch off with some mindless TV. Less than three minutes later, you jump up, realising the washing still needs to be hung out and the dog is scratching at the door needing an overdue ablutions walk.

You give in to the urge to check your work emails just before bed and answer an email requesting urgent information for a morning deadline.

You get to bed late and exhausted. You feel stressed about work and guilty about the lack of quality time you have spent with your family, and you berate yourself for not fitting in exercise.

Your alarm clock rings at 5.30 am and, after hitting snooze a couple of times, you have missed your morning walk (again) and are rushing to get the household prepared, packed and out the door...

In our race for more, we are reducing ourselves to less. And, for many of us, our health and wellbeing is the 'less', and the 'more' is an endless cycle of busyness, pursuit and stress.

The reality is that wellbeing isn't a nice-to-have: it is necessary. It is necessary for our health, energy, connection, creativity, relationships, performance… and the list goes on.

But despite this, we aren't getting our wellbeing right.

Lifestyle diseases like depression, anxiety and type 2 diabetes are skyrocketing around the world, and they are affecting people like you and me. In any one year, one in five of us is not doing okay, to the point where we have a diagnosable illness. Mental illnesses such as depression are outstripping cancer and heart disease as the leading cause of global disability.

Even our scientific community and health organisations don't have agreed definitions for wellbeing, wellness, resilience and happiness. It is pretty hard to improve something we can't define!

At the same time, we are drowning in a sea of information pollution on wellbeing. We are struggling to find fresh air and clear water and float up above the rubbish. Why focus on resilience? Think of resilience as the mask, snorkel and flippers that will help propel you to the surface.

Put simply, being more resilient both increases and sustains wellbeing.

This book is for real people facing real-time challenges every day. It provides simple, quick-start, evidence-based practical steps for wellbeing that works.

It's important to know that this book is NOT:

- a hero story of triumph over unimaginable odds
- a lesson from an elite group of soldiers on how to be the toughest and best
- a scientific or academic journal article on how the results of wellbeing interventions impact college students in the USA
- a directory of expert health or specialist medical advice, or a list of all the wellbeing and resilience strategies and skills that exist.

Instead, this book comes from the heart and head. It has emerged from trial and error: from my personal journey living with high-functioning anxiety, battling a sleep disorder and experiencing out-of-control stress that led to burnout. It has emerged from formal learning and continuous consultation with academics, from medical tests and consultations with a range of health professionals, and from the wisdom and traditions of the yogis.

It also comes from you – from the many interactions I have had over the last ten years in coaching conversations and change and resilience group training discussions, learning which of the strategies work best for you.

It is designed to cut through the clutter and provide you with a curated selection of evidence-based strategies that will help you move forward – to help you draw a line in the sand, take back control of your wellbeing and make different choices that are healthy and helpful for you.

It is an invitation to pause, reflect and recalibrate.

Call it personal development, self-help, self-development, professional development, leadership skills – I don't care! What matters is what you care about.

Resilience is a way for you to get more wellbeing, and this is what I know works to build resilience.

HOW TO USE THIS BOOK

This book will feel a lot like common sense – because it is. It is deliberately streamlined to propel you to make positive change.

For wellbeing to work, you must actually do some work!

You don't receive six-pack abdominal muscles as soon as you finish reading an article on how to get a flat stomach.

You don't get a fresh, warm, fragrant loaf of bread by googling bread-making instructions. Even if you decide to procure bread from someone else, you still need to make that decision, go to the shop, pay for it and transport it home.

You don't get a flourishing garden of vegetables by reading the instructions on the back of a packet of seeds.

You need to plant your seeds.

What you get from planting your seeds is the potential for bounty beyond your imagination. Who would think that from just five minutes of watering and nurturing seeds for 21 days, shoots of hope and life will spring up? With regular attention, those tiny shoots will turn into resilient seedlings that will continue to grow under all elements. The mix of water, sunlight, shelter, fertiliser and attention you add will influence the speed, hardiness and abundance of your nourishing vegetables.

This is a practical book in which you complete short activities as you go. The more activities you do, the more seeds you plant, the greater the clarity you will have on what is important to you, and the more relevant the content will be to you and what you need.

Not all seeds will turn into shoots; not all seedlings will transform into vegetables. But some will. The more you experiment, the more you learn about what works and what doesn't. And over time, your garden grows and flourishes.

This book gives you the knowledge and instructions, and the Resilience Recipes community can give you fertiliser in the form of a downloadable workbook and encouragement through our group programs.

The good news is that you don't need to complete the whole book before you start experiencing benefits. The awesome thing about wellbeing, that research shows, is that the simple act of talking to someone about your wellbeing is, in and of itself, a boost to your wellbeing!

So, I invite you to start by planting one seed: deciding upon and defining what wellbeing means to you in chapter one, and then talking about it with those closest to you.

Take this book at your own pace. Each chapter is designed to build on the last, but this book doesn't have to be worked through sequentially. If one area resonates with you more, go there, read it and commit to an action.

What we do know for sure is that without planting some of the seeds, nothing will grow. It's no good to read this book, understand it and then do… nothing.

Let's go!

PART I

TOO MANY COOKS

IN THE MEDIA, terms like wellbeing, wellness, mental health, resilience and self-care are all used interchangeably and jumbled in together. There is a plethora of information and misinformation spread across a range of platforms that is presented with confidence but without filtering or fact checking.

So, it isn't surprising that we've become stuck in overwhelm. Or that we've become cynical about work-provided wellness programs that don't work. Or that we chop and change rather than committing the necessary time to activities when something new hits the market.

Many of us are looking for a one-size-fits-all approach to wellbeing. We lose motivation when something doesn't work. Which doesn't make sense. Each one of us is unique, so our wellbeing and resilience recipes need to be unique too. No two people have the exact same values, beliefs, life circumstances, priorities or dreams.

In Part I we will step through what wellbeing means to you and identify the resilience recipe that will work best for you.

CHAPTER 1

THE WELLBEING WORRY

It started with me staying back late at work one night to meet a deadline. Then I began working late every Friday night, to clear my plate and my head so that I could relax on the weekend. This then turned in to 6 am starts every Monday morning so that I could get my week set up before everyone else came into the office. I didn't notice when 80-hour working weeks became my new norm. During the global financial crisis, every task became a priority, and every decision became the difference between someone having enough work versus losing their job. I stopped sleeping, because my overactive mind was on a 24/7 problem-solving cycle. Living with exhaustion and surviving on adrenalin, caffeine and sugar made getting out of bed each morning a battle. I was at the doctor's every week with a cold, stomach pains, headaches or skin inflammations. I was constantly irritated, quick to anger and easily upset, with unbalanced moods.

However, the blood tests came back month after month saying that I was in the 'normal range'. It took two years of living like this before I found a holistic doctor who gave me a diagnosis of adrenal exhaustion, leaky gut syndrome – and burnout. It took another two years of hard work to get back to being well.

Our busy lifestyles aren't working anymore. Globally, lifestyle diseases such as depression and anxiety have overtaken heart disease and cancer as the leading causes of disability. Nowadays, at any given point in time, one in five people is living with a mental illness.

We don't need to hit burnout or wait for total collapse to improve the way we live and increase our wellbeing.

So, what to do?

FIGHT OR FLIGHT?

Our bodies can't tell the difference between a real or imagined threat, or a major or minor stress. Our busy lifestyles are keeping us in a constant fight-or-flight state, continuously pumping out adrenalin and cortisol. We are living in our sympathetic nervous system (SNS) – wired and overtired as we attempt to 'do it all'.

Change is happening faster, more frequently and more dramatically than we are used to. Neurologically, we are wired to view change as a threat.

Experiences like the COVID-19 pandemic disrupt how and where we work, which brings uncertainty and stress for many, and the potential for burnout for those trying to manage it all.

Our brains like certainty. They are designed to predict and anticipate what will happen next. They continuously look for patterns or 'prescriptions' that make it easy to see what comes next and to run as much of our mental system on autopilot as they can.

Cast your mind back to when you first learnt to ride a bike. It was a mammoth task just staying upright! Eyes ahead, foot slipping off the pedal, other toe on the ground balancing you, pushing off, both feet up, wobbles, trying to avoid people, veering off course, trying to avoid the tree, heart thumping, squeezing hard on the brakes, skidding stop, foot down, bike topples. Rinse and repeat.

While learning to ride a bike was an exciting rite of passage, it could also be a stressful, exhausting and slow learning experience with constant challenges to your safety.

Now, years later, take a moment to replay in your mind the last time you rode a bike to do an errand. You probably don't recollect much of the experience between wheeling the bike out, heading off and then arriving at your destination. Riding a bike now feels hardwired into your subconscious, only interrupting your conscious mind occasionally if there is a hazard or potential danger.

When patterns play out the way we expect, our brain experiences a reward – ease and flow.

When patterns do not play out the way we expect, our brain experiences a threat and needs extra processing time and energy for vigilance. And our brain doesn't naturally distinguish between an immediate urgent danger, like our caveman ancestors fleeing for their lives from a sabre-toothed tiger, and the worry of missing an important deadline for our boss.

So, we are wired to find ambiguity and uncertainty distressing, because it means we cannot rely on our typical patterns to predict what will happen next. This gives us a sense of lacking control and can trigger our fear response. When we face significant uncertainty and feel that too much is out of our control, we can experience high levels of stress.

We want good balance, health and wellbeing, but stay stuck frantically pedalling our hamster wheel and juggling multiple balls in the air.

We rarely shift back to a state of calm, to rest and replenish before the next amygdala hijack.

We are running highly complicated and busy lives with caveman neurological operating systems. No wonder we are getting run-down and burning out!

Many of us recognise that we can't operate like this anymore, that we need to take control of our health and wellbeing. We can do this by reassessing our values and priorities and developing our resilience skills.

It is up to us to take charge of our lives and wellbeing. So, the question is:

Are you the driver, or a passenger on someone else's bus?

NO ONE-SIZE-FITS-ALL APPROACH

Google 'how do I improve my wellbeing?' and around 149 million results are returned. So, how can we know what to do when we're given so much information – and misinformation – about wellbeing?

First, we start with the definition of wellbeing, and then we build a plan to improve it. Sounds simple, doesn't it? Not really.

There is no consensus across health bodies or among academics around a single definition of wellbeing.

The word 'wellbeing' is used in many places and in many different ways. Some definitions emphasise feeling good, while others stress meaning, purpose or functioning well. And the terms 'wellbeing', 'quality of life' and 'happiness' are often used interchangeably.

Then there is the multitude of factors that influence wellbeing. Think of your own life. The way you feel and function is most likely affected by what's going on with your friends, family, health, financial circumstances and the level of choice you do or do not have in certain situations.

Wellbeing to a mum with a brand-new baby will most likely involve more sleep and help around the house. Wellbeing for an 18-year-old starting their first full-time job will be about the mastery of work skills and fitting into social networks.

So, people tend to describe wellbeing broadly in terms of domains, areas, descriptions, or examples of when, why or how they experience wellbeing. It is often easier to provide a list of parts of life that are important to our wellbeing – things like income, education, work, family and community life, values, environment, and physical and mental health.

It is also important to understand that wellbeing is not static. It exists on a continuum, where starting points differ, experiences are personal and wellbeing moves in a dynamic process. For example, a student's wellbeing can shift significantly during a week of delivering assignments and sitting for exams.

With so many moving parts, your wellbeing can change from one moment to the next. For example, if you are under a lot of stress at work, your wellbeing might be better at home than in the workplace.

What's more, wellbeing is subjective.

No two people have the exact same values, beliefs, life goals or personality traits, so certain aspects of wellbeing may be more or less important to one person than they are to another.

A senior executive working 70-hour weeks may rate getting home early during the week to spend time with their kids as a high wellbeing priority. A new mum returning to work may value the opportunity to do an interesting project with flexible hours working from home.

This is why my favourite formal definition of wellbeing is from Michaelson and Mahony in *Measuring Well-being: A guide for practitioners*: 'how people feel and how they function both on a personal and social level, as well as how they evaluate their lives as a whole'.

There is no one-size-fits-all approach to wellbeing. A personal trainer will emphasise physical health and provide wellbeing advice on fitness, exercise and often nutrition. A counsellor may focus on the mental health or relationship aspects of wellbeing. An executive coach will focus on work and career support. A workplace wellbeing program may focus on moving more via a step count competition or lunchtime yoga.

Many of us hope or expect a one-size-fits-all approach to wellbeing, and when we don't find it quickly, we give up.

When you go to a café to get lunch, you don't ask for a serve of lunch. You choose a sandwich, or perhaps a salad. You select a protein and a combination of other fillings like salad ingredients or cheese. You add seasoning, your favourite dressing and maybe some condiments, such as mustard.

A standard pre-made lunch may be good enough, but a freshly prepared meal with your favourite ingredients in just the right proportions is mouth-watering and can transform your afternoon. And your perfect lunch combination will be different to the person next to you.

Hence, the best definition of wellbeing is yours.

YOUR INDIVIDUAL WELLBEING ASSESSMENT

Often people will describe their need for improved wellbeing as better 'work-life balance'. I don't find this a helpful framework for a couple of reasons.

First, it is a black-and-white statement. Either-or assessments only provide a one-dimensional rating of what is a personal, nuanced view. Judging by tipping a work-life scale means you are forced into a bucket of either 'you have it' or 'you don't'. You have either got it right or wrong, and the scales are loaded towards the extremities, which very rarely balance.

At any point in time, we are all experiencing some level of well-being, and there are usually some parts of our lives that are working well. But the either-or approach doesn't recognise positives or small wins.

Second, looking at wellbeing through a balance lens assumes there are only two parts to our wellbeing scale: work and life (or work and home).

So, taking a scales approach doesn't reflect our unique and differing needs or values, or take into account shifts in our priorities.

The best definition of wellbeing is yours. That's why it is important to work out what wellbeing means to you and be able to apply it in a way that is meaningful.

So, before you set out on making some changes to your life, you first have to decide what wellbeing looks like for you.

In this chapter, we will work through four simple steps and a helpful framework to understand what contributes to your happiness, health and wellbeing.

Rather than a scale, think of your wellbeing as a wheel, or a pie, or a flower, where the aspects of wellbeing that are important to you are included in the segments. There are some evidence-based resources that support this approach.

Figure 1 shows the eight aspects or domains of wellbeing that are important to me.

Figure 1: The wellbeing wheel

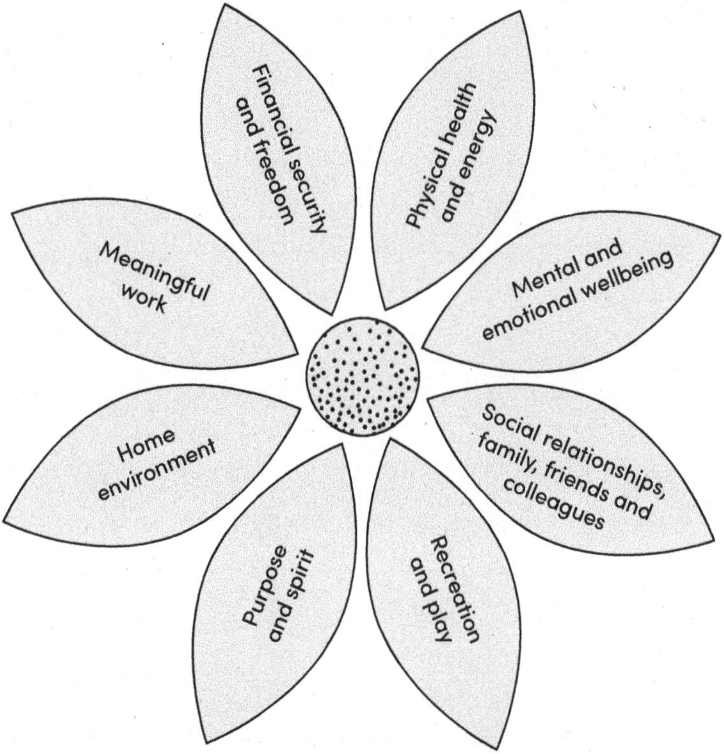

Here are my domains and definitions:

1. **Physical health and energy** means having the fitness, flexibility, strength and health to create and live my best life.
2. **Mental wellbeing** means managing my thoughts and mental chit-chat to be helpful and supportive, instead of getting stuck in a downward spiral of negative storytelling and self-criticism. **Emotional wellbeing** means having a healthy balance of positive and negative emotions, and bolstering my mood.

3. **Social wellbeing** means having a mix of family, friends and colleagues who boost my energy, who I can ask for help, and who will accept me regardless of how I show up and help me to be a better person. It means having mutually loving, generous and respectful relationships.
4. **Recreation and play** means a mix of rest, time out, adventures, creativity, lightness, discovery and playfulness.
5. **Purpose and spirit** means aligning what I do with my vision of making the world of work a better place. When the going gets tough, I know that my energy, care and time is worth it.
6. Having a light-filled, warm, welcoming and nurturing **home environment** gives me a safe place to retreat from the world to replenish and soothe my soul.
7. **Meaningful work** means work that makes a positive contribution to people's lives. The achievement of figuring out new and better ways of interacting with the world is motivating.
8. **Financial security** for me represents **freedom** – freedom from worry, freedom of options and choices, and freedom to choose where I spend my time.

My personal definition of wellbeing is: 'feeling good, functioning well, living with purpose, having fun and positively contributing'.

So, before we go any further, it's your turn to assess which six to eight areas in your life are important to you and how you feel.

Step 1: Identify what's important to you

Limiting yourself to somewhere between six and eight areas of wellbeing will bring you clarity and enable you to focus.

Identify the domains of wellbeing that are important to you. Write them on Figure 2.

Figure 2: Your personal wellbeing wheel

Then write your personal definition for each domain:

Area 1: ______________________________

____

____

Area 2: ______________________________

____

____

Area 3: ______________________________

____

____

Area 4: ______________________________

____

____

Area 5: ______________________________

____

____

Area 6: ______________________________

____

____

Area 7: ______________________________

____

____

Area 8: ______________________________

____

____

For extra ideas and inspiration, here are some popular wellbeing domains:

- Friends and social connectedness
- Family and relationships
- Lifestyle behaviours, such as daily exercise and regular sleep
- Emotional health
- Mental health
- Physical health and fitness
- Finances
- Meaningful work and career
- Sense of value and purpose
- Contribution to others, such as volunteering or giving
- Personal growth and learning
- Creativity
- Spirituality or religiosity
- Community
- Climate and nature.

Step 2: Rate how well you think you're doing

Taking the time to define what is important to you and rate how well you are living your priorities gives you greater self-awareness and more opportunities to make different choices.

Rate how satisfied you are with each of your domains of wellbeing on a scale from 1 to 10 on Figure 2.

To provide a guide on how to approach your rating, I suggest 1 means deeply unsatisfied, 5 means a neutral state and 10 means flourishing. It is important to apply your rating scale consistently to each of your wellbeing domains.

Here are some reflection questions to consider when assigning your ratings:

What is present when you are at your happiest?

What conditions are in play when you experience flow – when you are lost in the moment and lose sense of time?

What values are being met when you are happy?

What values are not being met when you are unhappy?

What are the dynamics going on when you feel dissatisfied, unhappy or miserable?

Step 3: Clarify your strengths and weaknesses

Identifying the areas of your wellbeing that are strengths and those that need attention will provide you with direction and clarity for your wellbeing definition and plan.

Based on your ratings, identify and write down:

- Your top two or three sources of wellbeing strength.
- The one or two areas of wellbeing that you would like to give more attention to.

Your sources of wellbeing strength:

1. ______________________________

____

____

2. ______________________________

____

____

3. ______________________________

____

____

Your wellbeing areas needing attention:

1. ______________________________

____

____

2. ______________________________

____

____

Human beings come with an inbuilt negativity bias, with our brains constantly scanning the environment for potential risks, dangers and threats, ready to activate our fight-or-flight system and keep us safe. So, we have a natural tendency to look for what is wrong, missing or not going well and we focus on the gaps.

However, we learn best and are more likely to experience flow and accomplish more by focusing on what is working, seeing best practice modelled and using our strengths. Research shows that leveraging our strengths builds positive emotions, which in turn opens up possibilities, builds confidence and increases wellbeing.

So, I encourage you to take stock of the aspects of wellbeing that are working well for you and list as many strengths and resources that you have at your disposal as possible.

Conversely, dwelling on what isn't working can trigger a downward spiral of negative thinking, narrowing our pathways and perspectives. So, just choose the one or two wellbeing gaps that are most important for you to improve.

Leveraging our strengths builds positive emotions, which in turn opens up possibilities and increases our options for improving wellbeing.

Step 4: Define your wellbeing

Now have a go at creating your definition of wellbeing.

There is no right or wrong, just a stake in the sand that you can start from. As your understanding of what is important to you evolves, feel free to come back and edit your definition of wellbeing as many times as you want.

Your definition of wellbeing:

Now that you have chosen the areas of wellbeing that are most important to you, rated your satisfaction with each area and created your wellbeing definition, it is time to decide what you want to do about it.

YOUR WELLBEING COMMITMENT

Imagine you are trying to fit a mix of big rocks, pebbles and sand into an empty jar.

If you start filling the jar by first adding the sand and then the pebbles, you will not have room for your rocks.

The big rocks symbolise the things that are the most important in your life. They represent the things that have real value: your health, your family, your partner. Even if everything else (the pebbles and the sand) was lost and only they remained, your life would still have meaning.

The pebbles represent the things in your life that are meaningful and matter but are not as critical, such as your job, house and hobbies.

The sand represents everything else, the small stuff: material possessions, chores and filler things such as watching television or browsing social media. These things don't mean much to your life as a whole and are more like time fillers.

I look at sand in two ways:

1. the internal blocks that you think, feel or do that stop you from focusing on what is important
2. the external demands or barriers that take up your time or resources.

Internal blocks could include procrastination, time-wasting activities or limiting beliefs about your value or abilities. External demands or barriers include the commitments you make to others.

Some of these activities serve us, like spending Saturday at our kids' sport. We have chosen to forgo personal time because it supports our prioritisation of family. But some of our activities don't serve us, such as a tendency to stay late at the office fixing someone else's work because they rush their tasks and make errors so they can get home early.

Take some time to list your key blocks and barriers. This will help you better identify and make choices about the sand in your life.

Your internal blocks:

1. ______________________

____

____

2. ______________________

____

____

3. ______________________

____

____

4. ______________________

____

____

Your external barriers:

1. ______________________________

____

____

2. ______________________________

____

____

3. ______________________________

____

____

4. ______________________________

____

____

Cast your mind back to how you defined wellbeing and rated the areas of wellbeing that are important to you. How does your wellbeing jar look?

If you start by putting sand and pebbles into the jar, you will not have room for rocks. This holds true with the things you let into your life. If you spend all your time on the small and insignificant things, you will run out of room for the things that are important.

Not everything can have the same priority, so you need to be deliberate about your two or three big rocks and be honest about what should be your sand.

Do you need to prioritise your health and wellbeing differently? What is the balance between your big rocks and your sand?

What are your big rocks? What are your pebbles?

Are your rocks covered in your wellbeing domains?

Are there pebbles that are hijacking your wellbeing?

What is the sand that is getting in your eyes and blurring your focus?

On a rating of 1 to 10, what is your commitment to making a positive change to your wellbeing?

○ 1 ○ 2 ○ 3 ○ 4 ○ 5 ○ 6 ○ 7 ○ 8 ○ 9 ○ 10

1 = deprioritise; 4 = do nothing; 5 = plan to change; 6 = start small; 10 = full steam ahead.

QUICK BITE

1. Be clear on your definition of wellbeing. You can't improve it unless you know what it is!
2. Identify and prioritise your wellbeing rocks.
3. Deprioritise your energy drainers and your investment in the busyness of the sand.

RESILIENCE RECIPE #1

WELLBEING THAT WORKS

A small, tight-knit, high-performing factory team of 45 people located on the outskirts of Melbourne, Australia, struggled with seasonal blues every year. In the winter months, people arrived at work in the dark, the days were grey and working on the lines was cold work. And this was reflected in the team's low mood and energy, occasionally punctuated by bursts of irritation and bickering.

The factory manager, Cameron, was part of the resilience and leadership training program I was running across the company to support healthy high performance and address burnout. Cameron asked me to run a wellbeing workshop with his team to show that the business cared about them.

We reorganised the canteen area into small break-out tables, brought in a projector and speakers, and spent the morning talking about wellbeing. Initially there was skepticism about allocating three hours to feelings.

We discussed the research for how good wellbeing levels boost personal relationships, energy, creativity, innovation and productivity. Then we moved on to a series of short wellbeing exercises. Each person spent five minutes reflecting on what wellbeing meant to them. They then took turns sharing their definitions with their small groups. And as they spoke, the energy in the room bubbled up.

Then each group, with a set of coloured markers, drew on butcher paper a collective picture of what wellbeing meant to them. A spokesperson for each small group presented their wellbeing artwork to the full factory team, who asked questions and engaged in the sharing. They covered the canteen wall with their wellbeing pictures.

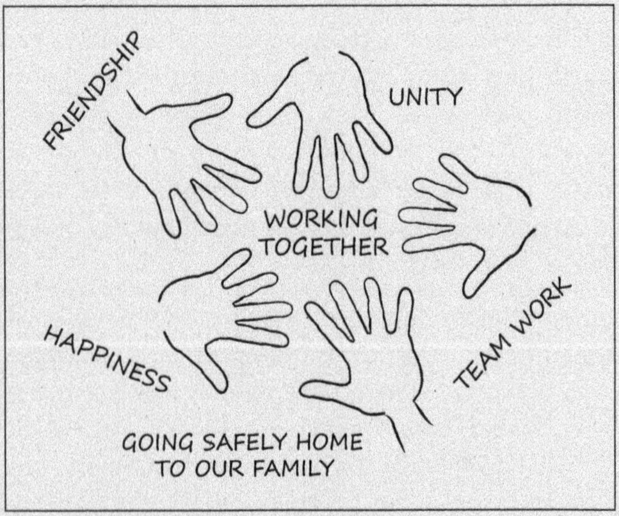

Cameron called me two weeks later to share that the place was still buzzing with energy. Their wellbeing pictures stayed up on the canteen walls, and they maintained their collective positive mood and goodwill throughout the full bleak winter season.

Why wouldn't you invest a few minutes to map out and share what wellbeing means to you when there is such a huge pay-off?

CHAPTER 2

RESILIENCE TO THE RESCUE

You're under pressure, exhausted from poor sleep and working long days dealing with a high-stakes, tight-deadline project that has you constantly stressed and wound up. Someone lets you down at a critical point in the project, and your blood boils – you snap at them.

The shock and fear on their face is a sign for you to stop, but you can't. Your rage spills forth even though a tiny voice inside your head tells you that you will regret this later.

The incident continues to consume your thoughts, hijacking your productivity for the rest of the day. You can't wait to get home and alleviate some of the pressure you are feeling in private. You walk in the front door and your partner demands your attention on something, and your reply is abrupt and harsh. You know you have wounded them. Guilt bites at you, but you have no energy left in the tank to regroup, and you get defensive and find criticisms to throw at your partner to deflect your crummy behaviour.

You are at the end of your tether, but sleep eludes you. You are worrying yourself sick over failing points of the project, bridges you are burning with key relationships at work and the damage inflicted to your personal relationship. You wish you could rewind the clock but feel as though you are spiralling out of control.

A strong resilience skill set would enable you to take back control of your actions and reactions at any point in this story.

Understanding your emotional triggers and the skills you can use to regulate your emotions would enable you to act rather than react. Being able to create mental space and clarity for your thoughts would give you more flexibility of behaviour when under stress. Investing in energy-building practices and activities would give you more fuel in the tank to draw from when you are running a physical health deficit such as lack of sleep.

So, instead of succumbing to the bumps in the road that can disrupt and derail you, with resilience you can make better, more helpful and healthy choices that continue to build your wellbeing.

You have more control over your health and wellbeing than you give yourself credit for. Take your control back.

WELLBEING HIJACKERS

In my experience mentoring and training hundreds of leaders, some of the top hijackers of our wellbeing are:

- Pressure and stress
- Fear and uncertainty
- Change and adversity.

Working back late at night to meet a deadline, all of your energy and willpower is focused on completing an important project report. You stress-eat chocolate and chips and fuel up on coffee, helpless to stop even though you know you will be beating yourself up for your health hijack the next day.

There are rumours of an impending restructure, and you are consumed with worry that your job is at risk. Rationally you know the best thing you can do in this situation is to demonstrate your value by over-delivering your current project. But you get caught up in speculation gossip with other colleagues, lose the motivation to work and get stuck in a self-fulfilling spiral of underperformance.

This is often the point where you give up, because it feels all too hard.

What is happening is that the 'freeze' part of your fear response kicks in, shutting down your ability to see different perspectives and alternative pathways for moving forward. Ever heard the expression 'we can't see the wood for the trees'?

Think of a 150-year-old tree that, despite existing in a harsh climate, consistently reaches for the sky. It grows faster and stronger with sunlight, rain and nutrient-rich soil. During drought, it sends roots down and deep into the earth for stability, and to find every drop of moisture. In a storm, it bends and flexes in the wind.

The tree bends, flexes, adapts and optimises energy in the face of unpredictable external elements and constant change. With resilience, the tree consistently grows in health and wellbeing, regardless of what challenges life throws at it.

With clarity on your own definition of wellbeing and which areas of wellbeing are of highest value to you, you now have something to work towards. But the journey to wellbeing isn't neat and straight – it's messy, just as real life is messy and complicated.

You need to be able to weather the turbulence and storms as they arise, which is where resilience comes in.

FRAMING RESILIENCE

The issue with resilience is that, like wellbeing, it is a term that is often misused, misunderstood and overused, particularly by politicians and other leaders.

Like wellbeing, resilience does not have a one-size-fits-all definition or recipe.

I tend to find that people fall into three categories when the word 'resilience' is mentioned: those who love it, those who roll their eyes when they hear it and those who have had a bad experience with it. If you fall into one of the latter categories, please bear with me, because the benefits of resilience significantly outweigh the problems.

Like wellbeing, one of the greatest challenges to understanding resilience and its benefits is that there is no universally agreed definition or standard for measurement. A recent Google search on resilience returned 325 million results.

At the simplest level, think of resilience as your ability to positively adapt to change and adversity, like the tree in the example earlier.

Many of us have grown up with the myth that resilience is something you were either born with or you weren't, that you are either resilient or you aren't.

Traditionally, being resilient has been thought of as being tough, reliable, stoic and persistent. Conversely, people lacking resilience have often been labelled as oversensitive, overly emotional or temperamental.

Luckily, science has evolved, and while we know that character and environment play a strong role in our starting levels of resilience, we can also learn the skills to increase our resilience. We can develop it, get better at it and also build it as an internal resource to draw on when we need it.

When you increase your overall resilience, it's easier to continue doing your best under pressure and maintain a balanced approach to life. Ultimately, resilience skills support your overall health and wellbeing.

The good news with resilience is that while it may be tricky to figure out, we all have some resilience. And we can also learn to increase our resilience.

WHY WORKPLACE WELLBEING DOESN'T, WELL, WORK

One of the biggest challenges often shared with me is people's experiences with resilience courses and wellbeing programs that have not worked.

Workplace wellness programs in particular receive a bad rap. Usually, an organisational wellness activity is chosen to fit a budget and maximise staff reach, with the hope that it will attract participation, be engaging and improve health. But when it doesn't, it is written off as a failure.

Given that there is no one-size-fits-all definition of wellbeing, why would we expect a one-size-fits-all wellness program to meet our individual needs? Would we really expect a one-hour lunchtime yoga class to reduce the stress associated with an unrealistic workload? Or a nutrition lecture to create lasting change in someone's physical health?

Research shows that resilience skills training can be effective in improving our health, wellbeing and performance. We just need to choose the right resilience strategies for our wellbeing goals.

So, the activities we choose to develop our wellbeing need to be fit for purpose. A helpful resilience skill for managing stress in healthy ways is emotional agility. Mental adaptability can help us switch off. Optimising energy helps us prioritise improvements to our physical wellbeing.

Resilience skills training works when it is fit for purpose.

MAKING RESILIENCE WORK FOR YOU

You may think your resilience is low because you get burnt out sometimes. But actually, you might be great in moments of high stress when others would crumble – or vice versa. That's because you can be naturally stronger in one area of resilience than another.

My personal resilience strengths are in dealing with pressure and adversity, but I struggle with sustaining mental and physical energy, which contributed to me experiencing burnout.

We are all born with resilience. It is just our starting levels that are different.

Resilience is individual in how it is experienced.

I define resilience as an internal resource for adapting positively to stress, supporting mental wellbeing during adversity and maintaining health and energy during prolonged uncertainty and change. The three 'superfoods' of resilience that are proven to improve wellbeing and work for me – emotional agility, mental adaptability and optimising energy – provide strong foundations for supercharging your wellbeing.

So, it is important that you choose the resilience strategies that support your values and wellbeing priorities. And this book will help you get started in making resilience right for you and your wellbeing.

Rather than a one-size-fits-all solution, I invite you to think of resilience as your ingredient list of superfoods. Different combinations will provide different tastes, fragrances, nutritional benefits and textures – a variety of recipe and menu options.

You need to choose the ingredients that are right for you and your journey.

Think of resilience as your recipe of superfoods to supercharge your wellbeing.

THE RESILIENCE ROADMAP

It is important to understand your resilience starting point in relation to your wellbeing. When you first learnt to drive a car, you didn't just jump into the car and start driving. Some of the new skills came easily, while others required focus and determination.

Developing resilience skills is like that.

Over time, your driving has become an automatic habit. Some of our automatic habits serve us, providing us with ease and safety, such as automatically slamming on the brakes to avoid hitting a dog that has run out onto the road. Other automatic habits don't serve us, such as running the petrol tank down so low that we create stress by having to urgently look for a service station when we don't have time to waste.

We all have aspects of resilience that are strengths, but we also have opportunities to develop resilience skills we may have neglected that could supercharge our wellbeing. When I hit burnout, I had been overly relying on my coping skills and not investing enough in energy and stamina.

When you first started learning to drive a car, your instructor assessed your starting point and developed a learning plan. You need to assess your wellbeing starting point in relation to your levels of resilience.

ASSESSING YOUR WELLBEING WITH A RESILIENCE LENS

Your starting level of wellbeing will determine the most useful set of resilience strategies for refuelling your tank.

So, let's start by assessing what your wellbeing starting level is.

I like to think of levels of wellbeing in relation to an hourglass. When we are feeling good and functioning well, there is more sand at the top than sand that has run through and needs replenishing. When we are feeling depleted or have more of our domains of wellbeing needing attention than giving us strength, we are at a deficit.

I assess wellbeing using five levels, as illustrated in Figure 3. Let's look at each level in turn.

Figure 3: Wellbeing levels

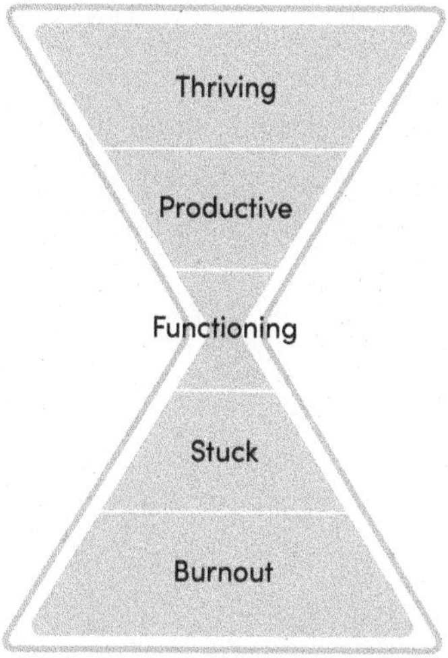

1. Burnout

If you are or in Burnout mode, your energy is drained, your motivation is sluggish and moving forward with your work feels hard.

2. Stuck

Stuck can quite literally feel like you are stuck in a rut or caught mindlessly running on a never-ending hamster wheel. Here, your mojo is flat, and possibly more is feeling wrong than right. And the constant demands on your time and task list may feel out of control and insurmountable.

3. Functioning

At Functioning, it feels like you are coping with everything thrown at you – just. You are getting everything done that you need to, but the pace feels unrelenting. You are able to catch a breath now and then but often feel like you can't see the wood for the trees.

4. Productive

The Productive level is where you are performing, achieving well and moving forward with your projects and goals. The constant busyness is manageable, but you are burning through your energy.

5. Thriving

At Thriving, life has the right mix of enjoyment, accomplishment, effort and ease.

Where you are at and how you are feeling about your wellbeing will help you select the resilience ingredients that will be most useful for your unique wellbeing recipe.

Using Figure 4, choose your starting point or current level of wellbeing. Then, next to your rating, write why you have chosen your rating.

Figure 4: Your wellbeing level assessment

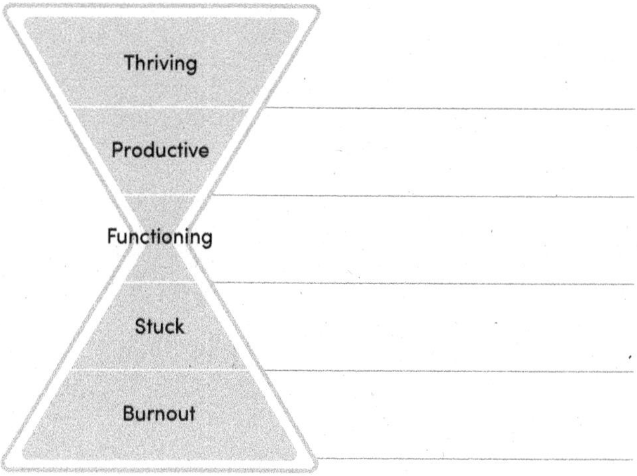

Consider the following reflection questions with your rating:

What is working well for you at present?

In what areas of your life do you feel at ease?

Are there any areas in which you are treading water?

How are your energy levels? Where are you getting energy from? What are your energy drainers?

What isn't working so well?

QUICK BITE

Choosing one resilience focus to develop that meets you where you currently are with your wellbeing is the best way to set yourself up for success.

As you grow in capability, confidence and energy, you can then layer on additional wellbeing boosts at a pace that works for you.

RESILIENCE RECIPE #2

RESILIENCE THAT IS RIGHT FOR YOU

A well-regarded, five-star hotel was struggling with the challenge of retaining and motivating good staff within the context of multiple owner changes and restructuring. The HR Director asked me for guidance on how to provide a wellbeing program that would boost engagement and show staff the business cared.

We started the conversation by discussing what wellbeing activities the hotel had already implemented. They had run some wellness activities, such as lunchtime yoga and a step activity challenge, but were disappointed with low participation and engagement.

I asked him what his key people challenges were. The Australian hospitality industry is characterised by a highly casual workforce of young people, which brings challenges of high staff turnover, lack of team cohesion and service inconsistencies. This hotel was no different.

We mapped out the most relevant wellbeing domains for the staff demographic. These included financial security, social inclusion and career development opportunities. When we went through the results of the latest cultural survey, the top concern for staff was a lack of belonging. Rotating rostered shiftwork 24 hours a day, seven days a week, with workers constantly on their feet supporting guests, meant they had little opportunity to connect and make friends.

With 80% of staff spending most of their time at work on their feet, they didn't need more physical wellness opportunities. They needed more opportunities to connect, to feel psychologically safe at work rather than isolated, and resilience skills training to help them better manage uncertainty and change.

Are you choosing the right resilience strategies for your wellbeing needs?

PART II

INGREDIENTS FOR CHANGE

INCREASING RESILIENCE is one of the best boosts for your wellbeing.

When you increase your overall resilience, it's easier to continue to do your best under pressure and maintain a balanced approach to life. Understanding where you are at and how you are feeling about your wellbeing will help you select the resilience ingredients that will be most useful for your unique wellbeing recipe.

Part II is where we transform knowing into planning, preparing and doing.

Assuming you have done the exercises in Part I, you will have decided what wellbeing means for you, rated where you currently are and chosen what to improve, and are ready to take the next step. Your wellbeing diagnostic work will pay off in making this next section flow faster and bring you greater clarity on what is right for you.

If you haven't done the wellbeing diagnostic exercises yet and you are doing a light skim, I recommend you read through this next part with a highlighter to mark the strategies that most resonate with you, then choose a strategy to try out for a quick wellbeing boost. Go back and work through Part I when you are ready.

Remember, building your resilience skills supports your overall health and wellbeing.

Research shows that resilience skills can be effective in improving your health, wellbeing and performance. You just need to choose the right resilience strategies for your wellbeing goals. You don't fill a car petrol tank with water. You don't fill the windscreen wipers with oil. You don't pump up the tyres with petrol.

I have given each of the stages of wellbeing an associated resilience focus. This takes the guesswork out of where to start and what will be the most effective wellbeing boost for where you are now. Remember Figure 4? In Figure 5, below, I have mapped the resilience focus for each wellbeing stage.

Figure 5: Stages of wellbeing with the resilience focus

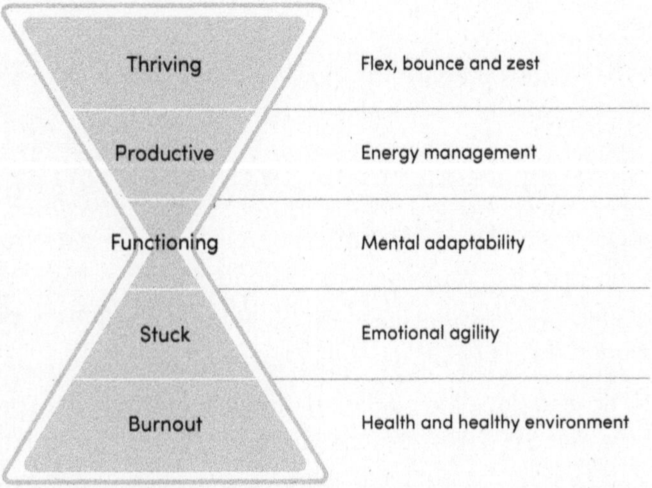

The activities you choose to support your wellbeing need to be fit for purpose. For example, a helpful resilience skill for dealing with stress or low motivation in a healthy way is emotional agility. To calm an overactive and busy mind that doesn't switch off, you might choose mindfulness from your mental adaptability toolkit. To improve stamina and increase your capacity to get things done, you would look for ways to optimise your energy.

If you are experiencing burnout, it is important that you seek professional medical help for your mental and physical health.

There are three key ingredients that make up the core of your resilience recipe, as shown in Figure 6.

Figure 6: Three resilience ingredients

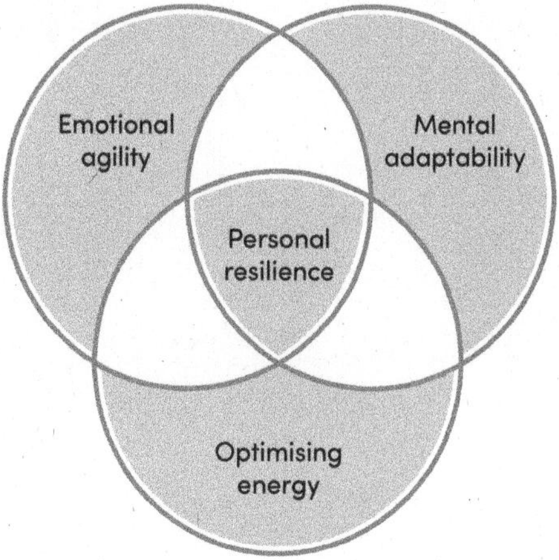

The ingredients are:

1. **Emotional agility:** to understand your emotional triggers and stress reactions and create the power to act, rather than react to emotional hijacks.
2. **Mental adaptability:** to take control of your mind and mood, instead of your busy mind and fake news holding you hostage.
3. **Optimising energy:** where you choose your appropriate balance and boundaries to sustain you for the long haul, rather than succumbing to the busyness treadmill and burnout.

We'll look at each of these in turn throughout Part II.

CHAPTER 3

EMOTIONAL AGILITY

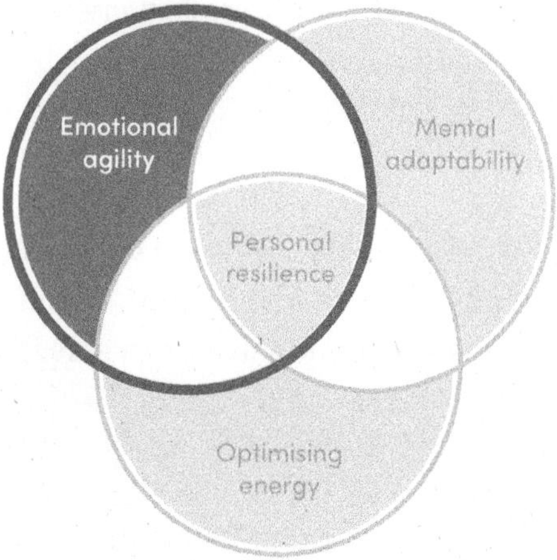

Most of us will have witnessed screaming toddlers at the shops reacting to being told no to the chocolate they desperately want. Their little minds and bodies are totally consumed with rage, their arms and legs lashing out, oblivious to anything else around them other than the person blocking them from getting what they want.

As we evolve into adulthood, our emotional regulation skills can still hijack us, toddler-style.

For example, a driver cuts you off in traffic, causing you to veer and hit your side mirror on a pole to avoid hitting them. They give you a casual wave and accelerate away, uncaring of the damage to your car resulting from their reckless behaviour. Consumed with rage, you stew, fume, tell and retell the story. You become your story, and it ruins your day. Or, consumed with rage, you race after them, tailgating them. They pull up at the lights, get out of their car and charge back to you with their fists up, ready to fight.

Getting emotionally hijacked and stuck in mental ruminations is one of the ways we activate our stress response. Getting 'hooked' by our thoughts and feelings can lock us into black-and-white opinions and behaviours that limit our ability to connect, solve and compromise.

Emotional agility is the ability to experience your thoughts and emotions in a helpful, values-aligned way, rather than becoming driven in a negative way.

Responding to the scenario above in an emotionally agile way might involve taking a photo of the offending car's number plate, pulling up to the side of the road and taking notes about the location, date, time and events, collecting witness accounts and lodging a police report, then choosing to put it behind you and move forward with the rest of your day.

ACT RATHER THAN REACTING

The key to making your life better is to stop blaming others for triggering reactions in you that you don't like. The problem is not what others do; it is your reaction to what they do.

Susan David, Harvard University expert and author of *Emotional Agility*, describes the skill of being emotionally agile as the ability to:

- recognise and accept your emotions before reacting and decide how you'd like to respond
- treat painful emotions when they arise as 'data points and signposts' that help you to identify and navigate the important problems and challenges in your life.

Ideally, you choose to respond in a way that aligns with your values and best interests, acting in ways that build bridges and create multiple pathways for connection, compassion, compromise and getting your needs met while also meeting the needs of others.

'Emotional rigidity', or the tendency to 'get hooked' by thoughts, feelings and behaviours that don't serve you, can destroy your wellbeing. Think again of the previous example and how all-consuming, blinding and destructive the feelings of road rage can be.

We can become stuck in a downward spiral of fear, anger or negative thoughts and feelings, which narrows our perspective and reduces options for solutions. And when we commit to our mental barriers and blocks, we can create disconnection and isolation, and inadvertently destroy wellbeing.

Emotional agility is a key resilience skill that can lower stress, broaden your perspective and support your emotional, mental and social wellbeing.

When you're able to create separation between yourself and what is happening around you, and choose how you act in response, you can cope better with complexity and challenges.

This isn't about turning off, suppressing or correcting negative or painful emotions, as this only tends to make you feel worse in the long run. Rather, it is about allowing yourself to experience and make space for the full range of your emotions.

RECIPES FOR RESILIENCE

Imagine that your mind is an ocean. Your thoughts and feelings move over the ocean's surface – they can be ripples, crashing waves or big storms. But no matter how big or turbulent the waves are, there is calmness at the bottom of the ocean.

Think of stormy feelings and emotions as surface level and temporary.

You can choose to stay caught up in the rips, the pull and churn of the waves, or you can choose to find the calmness on the ocean floor.

Developing emotional agility helps you to transform storms brewing on the horizon by dropping the winds and creating a more soothing ocean sunset.

There are three skills that make up emotional agility:

1. **Emotional awareness:** accurately identifying what you are feeling.
2. **Emotional regulation:** creating the space to identify and act rather than react.
3. **Broaden and build positive emotions:** practising the powers of gratitude and connection.

Let's look at each in more detail.

1. Emotional awareness

Emotional awareness is the ability to accurately understand your emotions and identify your emotional triggers.

People with emotional awareness understand what they're feeling and why. They also understand the feelings of others better because they are more in touch with their own inner life. This type of emotional understanding allows people to respond appropriately to others, and to better regulate and cope with difficult emotions such as anger or fear.

When someone asks how you are, what is your default answer? Well? Good? Busy? Tired? Fabulous? Fighting fit? Is your response a reflection of how you are, or is it a well-honed automatic response that you don't need to think about?

To develop your emotional agility, you need to investigate your automatic responses, tune into the layers of emotion beneath and listen to what they are telling you.

There is a big difference between 'I am well because I managed to conquer my depressive thoughts and get out of bed this morning' and 'I am well because I got a good night's sleep and am feeling relaxed'. And there is a big difference between the resilience strategies you would choose to support your wellbeing in those situations.

At the most basic level, our emotions can be classified into six groups or families: mad, sad, scared, peaceful, powerful and joyful, as shown in Figure 7 (overleaf).

We usually do our best to push our messy, challenging and uncomfortable emotions aside and get rid of them as soon as possible, but what you really need to do is acknowledge them and sit with them.

We don't often take the time to investigate our emotional data points to get a more accurate reading on the cause for why we may be feeling angry or irritated. Feeling angry because you are hurt by a friend's treatment of you is very different to feeling angry because you are frustrated with yourself for making the same silly mistake twice.

We all have emotional triggers – you know, the short fuses that explode quickly, as opposed to the long fuses that burn slow and can fizzle out. Our emotional triggers are often illogical, irrational, emotional and set off by those who are closest to us.

Think of your partner who leaves their wet towel on the carpet, your toddler who demands one more bedtime story an hour after they should be asleep, your neighbour practising the drums at 10 pm or your boss wanting a report that he has sat on to be urgently rewritten after you have already left work for the day.

Take a minute to pause and list as many of your emotional triggers as you can think of.

We tend to find it easier to connect with our negative emotions, so let's go with those. However, if positive emotional triggers spring to mind, like your partner bringing you a cup of tea in bed, please list those as well.

Next, we're going to use the wheel in Figure 7 to investigate some of your emotional triggers.

Figure 7: Wheel of common emotional descriptors

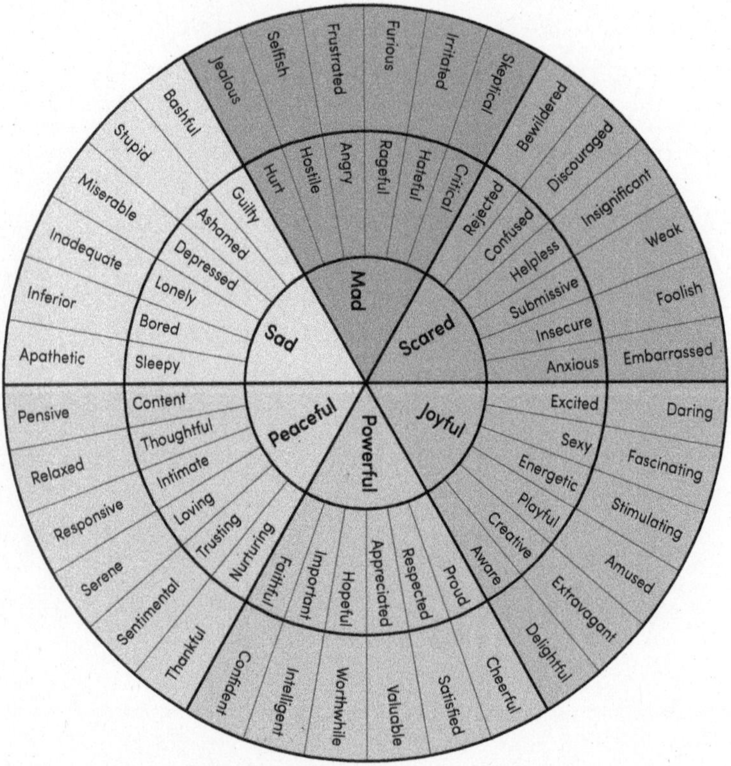

Let me give you an example. I asked my partner to come home at a specific time to help me prepare for a dinner party with friends. He arrived over an hour late and at the same time as our first guest. I was mad and upset. If I had stayed mad, I would have exploded at him and increased the emotional temperature for both of us.

I paused a moment to investigate the angry feeling and moved to the middle ring of the emotional wheel. Where did the anger come from? What was beneath the anger? I have an emotional trigger with being let down by people. I realised that what I was feeling was anxious, which is in the 'scared' family of emotions.

Finally, looking at the outer ring, I identified that I was feeling insignificant to my partner, that he had deprioritised me. And because I was now behind on the dinner party preparations, I felt embarrassed when the first guests walked into the kitchen that was still in a mess.

Spending the extra two minutes analysing my emotions enabled me to have a more constructive conversation with my partner, and gave both of us the opportunity to defuse the emotional situation. It gave him the space to apologise, make me and our guests a drink and then take responsibility for cleaning up the kitchen and give me a break from the preparations.

Accurately labelling emotions helps us create better signposting.

When you look at the wheel of common emotions in Figure 7, I invite you to highlight the most immediate or centre order emotions associated with your emotional trigger examples, for example angry, sad, anxious, scared, content.

If the emotions you are looking for aren't there, feel free to add them to the perimeter of the emotional family that feels like the best fit. For example, you might put 'upset' near the 'sad' set of emotions.

Now take a look at the more nuanced layers of emotions in the middle and then outer rings of the wheel. Choose the most specific and accurate responses that you could add to your emotional vocabulary, for example discouraged, lonely, overwhelmed, embarrassed.

And then consider the options that have now opened up for how you may respond the next time you feel triggered.

2. Emotional regulation

Secondly, emotional regulation is the skill to create space between your emotion and mental judgement and then to consciously act rather than react to emotional hijacks.

Learning to sit with your uncomfortable feelings, objectively look at what they are telling you and create space before acting is a powerful resilience skill.

When you feel your emotional temperature rising, with emotional regulation you can make the choice to turn down the heat to a bubbling simmer, rather than crank up the dial, put the lid on and encourage it to boil over.

Five steps to SNAPP

Learn to SNAPP rather than SNAP when you become emotionally triggered. This five-step process will help you create the space to act rather than react.

1. **Stop** what you are doing when you become emotionally triggered.

2. **Notice** what is happening in your body (temperature, tension, breathing) and in your mind (self-talk, stories, criticism), creating separation between the emotion and automatic meaning.

   For example, anxiety may sound like self-criticism over something you haven't done and feel like a cold sinking sensation in the pit of your stomach.

3. **Allow** the emotion to occur.

   - Take the time you need to accurately identify the emotion. Give what you are feeling a label.
   - Create separation between the emotion and your identity. You feel an emotion, you are not the emotion. It is one tiny fleeting expression of what makes up you, in that moment.

     'I am experiencing anger', or 'I am experiencing excitement' is more accurate than 'I am angry', or 'I am excited'.

   - Try not to judge the feeling or label as good or bad. This can add an extra layer of meaning that isn't helpful. Particularly for emotions that we don't like or don't want.

     Framing emotions that we don't like and don't want as challenging, messy, complicated or complex provides a lens that enables empathy, self-compassion and kindness.

- Assess what value has been triggered to create this emotional reaction in you. Often, we are triggered when our values are in conflict.

  For example, anger may more accurately be labelled as hurt. We are hurt because someone who knows us well may have unfairly accused us of doing the wrong thing, triggering values like loyalty, trust, fairness or justice.

4. **Pause** and breathe to create space between your emotion and (re)action.

   We have a powerful internal tool for bringing calm to our own system. Breathe. Slowly. And deeply.

   Short, quick chest breathing fuels our sympathetic nervous system (SNS) and promotes our fight or flight response. When we are experiencing an emotional hijack that upsets us our breathing will offer mirror our emotional state.

   Deliberate belly breathing with focus on long exhales taps into our parasympathetic nervous system (PNS) – promoting our rest-and-digest response which promotes calm. Just three to five minutes of slow deliberate breathing can bring an emotional, mental and physical re-set.

5. Then choose **purposeful** and compassionate action.

   There is a range of actions you can choose to respond with that don't involve an emotional outburst or saying or doing things you may regret later.

   For example:

   - Park it – to give you time to calm down and decide whether to put it down or pick it up later.
   - Peace – open up dialogue with options for multiple perspectives and pathways.

- Protest – develop a perspective and path of action that supports your values.
- Persist – acknowledge that your chosen path is tough but worth pursuing.

Learn to SNAPP rather than SNAP.

Now it is your turn.

When you feel your emotional temperature rising do you have a default reaction or response?

For example: explode, lash out, walk away, curl up into a ball, retreat into your shell.

How could adding SNAPP to your resilience toolkit support your wellbeing?

Considering the five steps to SNAPP:

Which of the steps do you do well?

Which step might be helpful for you to cultivate?

QUICK BITE

When you feel your emotional temperature rising, try a calming breath to switch you out of your SNS and into your PNS.

Gently close your eyes and sit in an upright but neutral position. Breathe in slowly and into your belly for the count of four. Puff your belly up with the air. Breathe out slowly and gently from your belly for a beat or two longer than your inbreath. Squeeze all the air out of your belly, until there is no more air left.

Do three to five rounds of calming breath.

3. Broaden and build positive emotions

Fear and strong negative emotions can trigger our fight or flight response, narrowing our thinking to focus only on what is necessary for our immediate survival. With our brain continuously scanning our environment for danger, risk and threat, it is easy for us to fall into patterns of looking for what is wrong, missing or not working, to focus on minimising potential negatives.

On the other hand, positive emotions can have the effect of broadening our awareness and response to events, as well as building our resiliency and coping skills.

As positive emotions don't have immediate survival value, they can have the effect of broadening our awareness and opening our mind, letting us see a bigger picture, be more creative and access more options for problem-solving.

Picture a waterlily. At night, when it is pitch black, the flower is closed up tight. As the sun starts to rise, the outer petals begin to open. With the brightening sun, the petals unfurl wider, and the world expands and becomes larger. Sunlight changes the openness of flowers.

The warmth of positive emotions changes how open our perspective is and enhances our ability to see a bigger picture and connect with others. The ten most common positive or warming emotions are joy, gratitude, serenity, interest, hope, pride, amusement, inspiration, awe and love.

University of North Carolina researcher Barbara Fredrickson's research found that people feel and do their best when they have a ratio of at least three times as many positive emotions as negative emotions.

Her studies showed that people who are high in resiliency experience more positive emotions even in the face of stress. And cultivating positive emotions can help you cope with negative emotions. Higher resilience then leads to increased wellbeing, which creates an upward spiral of continually improving wellbeing.

Deliberately developing our positive emotions builds our resilience and wellbeing.

Gratitude the superfood

Gratitude involves both feeling and expressing a deep sense of thankfulness to others; the sense of having been given a gift by that person or event. Research has long supported the importance of feeling gratitude and expressing our thanks in promoting health and happiness.

Gratitude also provides physical health benefits, such as improved cardiovascular and immune functioning. It has spiritual benefits as well, such as connectedness with life, a general sense of responsibility towards others and a reduced emphasis on material possessions.

And gratitude is simple, easy and costs nothing to cultivate.

- Writing down three things that you are grateful for, 21 days in a row, develops a new brain pattern for scanning the world for the positives before the negatives.
- Journalling about one positive experience you've had over the previous 24 hours enables your brain to relive it with the positive associated emotions.

- Creating a gratitude jar that you drop notes into about positive experiences as they occur enables you to return to and relive those experiences when you need a pick-me-up.

And it is easy to share gratitude with others through:

- random acts of kindness, such as buying another person a coffee or helping a neighbour
- starting your workday by writing one positive email praising or thanking somebody in your network
- encouraging each family member to share one thing they are appreciative of from their day over dinner.

The win-win of doing something kind for someone else is that it builds positive emotions in the giver as well as the receiver.

What is one small thing you will do each day to cultivate your gratitude?

____

____

____

____

____

Supercharge your social support

Not only does gratitude feel good for us, it also helps us build trust and closer bonds with the people around us.

When people witness an expression of gratitude, they see that the grateful person is the kind of person who notices when other people do kind things and takes the time to acknowledge them.

Gratitude not only improves our one-on-one relationships but can bring entire groups together. Simply witnessing an act of gratitude by someone else can inspire a desire to help and connect with people.

Building strong, supportive, positive relationships is not only a key foundation for our resilience, but social wellbeing is the number one contributor to our overall wellbeing.

Social wellbeing is the extent to which you feel a sense of belonging, social inclusion and social stability. It encompasses your lifestyle, values and beliefs, as well as feeling valued as a person, family member, friend and employee.

As human beings, we are wired to connect. A study done in Framingham, Massachusetts – a small town of 5000 people – showed that when someone became happy or sad, that emotion rippled through the town.

And our social wiring is so strong that social support is the number one promoter of our wellbeing, and the number one protective factor for our mental health.

Supercharge your social wellbeing by deliberately sharing positive emotions:

- Share a laugh with a friend.
- Show your love with a hug for those who are closest to you.
- Share a compliment or say thank you to someone in your network each day (yes, doubling down with gratitude).
- Organise a weekly walk and talk with your best friend.
- Take a colleague to an inspirational talk.

- Book a Zoom video coffee catch-up with geographically distanced family.
- Join a group that shares your interest – book club, walking group, trivia team, volunteering, art class, sporting group.
- Take your pet and a coffee to the local dog park to enjoy the playful antics with other dog owners.
- Take an active role in bettering your community – whether that be your neighbourhood, cultural affiliation, university society, church or social cause.

It is the quality of our connections, rather than the quantity, that counts the most with wellbeing.

What small rituals or activities will you focus on to supercharge your social wellbeing? Write down some examples of things you will do daily, weekly and monthly.

Daily: ______________________________

____

____

____

____

Weekly: ______________________________

____

____

____

____

____

Monthly: ____

____

____

____

____

____

____

____

____

____

____

A BUFFER FOR LIFE

Accurately identifying and accepting all of your emotions, even the messy ones, is the cornerstone of resilience. Creating the space to manage your emotions rather than allowing your emotions to hijack you gives you the ability to cope with whatever life throws at you.

Broadening and building your positive emotions builds your resilience, increases your wellbeing and provides you with a buffer for when life throws you a curve ball.

QUICK BITE

Here are some small, everyday tips to foster your emotional and social wellbeing:

- Start the morning with listing three things that you are grateful for to create happy endorphins.
- Set yourself a helpful intention each day, such as to learn something new, or to be present. Where you direct your focus, your energy follows.
- Choose to do something you love each day – spend an extra minute in your hot morning shower, or read fiction for 20 minutes – demonstrating to yourself that your wellbeing matters.
- Connect with one person who brings you joy, enhancing your social wellbeing.

Acknowledge the amazing human you are and the challenges you have successfully overcome in the past, and know you are capable of navigating this.

RESILIENCE RECIPE #3

BREAKING OUT OF A PIGEONHOLE

Adam was a mid-level public service manager who had worked within the same work area and team for ten years. He loved the organisation and people that he worked with, but was bored with the work and resentful of those around him achieving regular promotions and opportunities to do new work.

He joined one of my mentoring programs and was very vocal about his anger at being pigeonholed, his feelings of resentment and his negative impression of how promotions were managed. We worked through some self-reflection exercises and Adam realised that by blaming the system around him, he had fallen into a victim mentality and given away his power.

Each time he saw others in his team applying for new roles, heading off to interviews and having professional development conversations, it triggered strong, negative emotional reactions within him. His automatic interpretation was that he was being pigeonholed by the department. Good enough to stay stuck in the same role, but not good enough to be given a promotion. Taken for granted in the experience he shared in supporting others, but not valued enough to have the opportunity to gain new skills and experience.

Adam had always taken pride in his lack of filter and viewed the reactive sharing of his feelings as courageously sharing the truth. What he hadn't noticed over time was that his truth had become negative, complaining, draining and repetitive. Not only was he flattening his mood, he was driving away those around him.

In our mentoring sessions, Adam came to the powerful revelation that he was contributing to the pigeonhole that he was stuck in. He realised that the first change he needed to make was within himself. Instead of frustrated and negative, how did he want to feel? Instead of emotional explosions, how did he want to show up? Instead of continuously venting, how did he want to interact with others? And then he created a roadmap to develop the emotional agility that would move him from his default emotional state to where he wanted to be.

Adam identified his emotional triggers and the unhelpful stories he had been telling himself. He worked on pause-button strategies for creating space between his emotional reactions and verbal responses. He trained himself to ask more questions rather than leaping to conclusions. He became purposeful in his interactions with others. And then he created opportunities to give people a positive experience of his contribution, willingness to listen and desire for growth opportunities.

Six months later, Adam was given a project opportunity in a different work area with a new team. Twelve months later, he had achieved that elusive promotion, doing work he loved with people he liked.

Are you emotionally agile or emotionally stuck?
Are you putting your best foot forward?
Or are you being your own worst enemy?

CHAPTER 4

MENTAL ADAPTABILITY

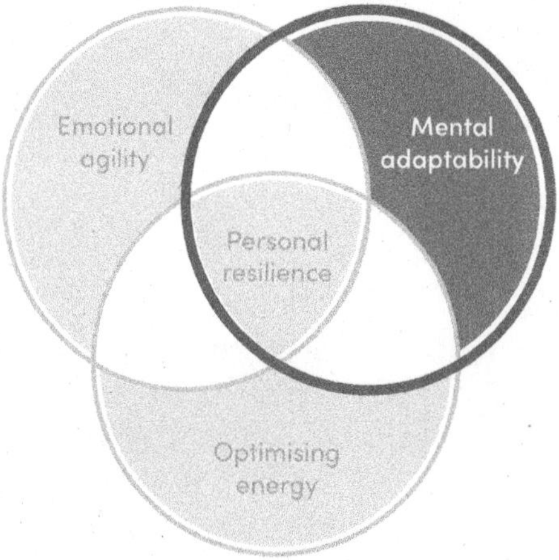

The story of the two wolves is a legend often attributed to the Cherokee people. An old wise Cherokee speaks to his grandson of the battle between the two wolves that goes on inside each of us.

'One wolf is dark and evil. This wolf is anger, jealousy, resentment, inferiority, criticism and sorrow. The other wolf is light and love. This wolf is love, peace, hope, kindness, empathy and compassion.'

The grandson thought about this for a couple of minutes and then asked his grandfather, 'Which wolf wins the fight?' The old wise Cherokee simply replied, 'The wolf I feed.'

This is usually where this story ends. But let's think this battle through.

If we ignore our angry wolf, we will end up in a long battle. We will be feeding that wolf's power and size with our hostility and fear. But if we pay attention to our angry wolf's emotional sign-posts, we can create the space of acceptance, which will enable us to stop fighting them.

We can also strengthen the loving wolf by giving it nourishment and support. We can do this by making regular practices of gratitude-sharing, movement and exercise, and relaxing with our loved ones. Our light wolf can become our strong, calm companion by our side as we journey through the ups and downs of life, soothing our dark wolf during the tougher times.

So, for our story let's share a couple of key ingredients and recipes that will help you accept the dark wolf and feed the light wolf.

WHO IS IN THE DRIVER'S SEAT?

While emotional agility helps us experience emotions in a useful, values-aligned way, mental adaptability helps guide the meaning you make and the actions you choose.

We have more control and choice over our light and dark wolves than we sometimes realise. Developing our mental adaptability will help with this.

Think of mental adaptability as the roadmap that contains your emotional data points and signposts.

Getting emotionally hijacked or stuck in negative thinking is like finding yourself on a one-way highway with no exits or turnoffs. Mental adaptability is your ability to see the broader terrain – the side streets and scenic roads, the intersections and bridges. The more you can see, the more options you have available to you.

In our rapidly changing environment, adaptability has never been more important. A high level of adaptability means you're generally better able to handle change successfully.

In line with the psychological flexibility literature, I define mental adaptability as the ability to adjust your thinking and take different perspectives in new or difficult situations to overcome obstacles, learn and grow, and improve your effectiveness. Adaptable people tend to be happier and more content as they're not struggling against the tide or trying to resist when things change.

So, mental adaptability is more than just coping with change – it's also having the confidence and emotional and mental mastery to remain calm and persist in the face of difficulties.

Mental adaptability works hand in hand with resilience. With mental adaptability, long periods of uncertainty and change are less likely to impact negatively on your overall personal wellbeing.

Mental adaptability means managing changing priorities, thinking on your feet, bouncing forward through life's challenges with a positive attitude and knowing that whatever happens, you will be okay.

GOING WITH THE FLOW

Being able to 'go with the flow' or be flexible in your thinking is a necessary skill for dealing with life's inevitable changes. However, for many people, this is much easier said than done. They are like an animal crossing the road at night that freezes instead of fleeing from the headlights of an oncoming car. Our brain likes certainty and patterns, and we can sometimes get fixed in our way of thinking and struggle to accept new ideas and adopt different ways of doing things.

We can get stuck in a loop of rumination where we can't seem to think about things in a different way. An example of this could be when a colleague takes our coffee mug at work, and our brain gets busy dredging up all the other things that person has done, reinforcing our view that they are out to get us. Instead, a more likely reality is that they think it is a communal coffee mug because it is in a shared kitchen cupboard.

Our brain remembers what we reinforce in our neural pathways, so if we're telling ourselves the same 'facts' or 'stories' all the time, we're stamping our neural pathways with them. This eventually becomes a self-fulfilling downward spiral of reduced flexibility to see other perspectives, which is the equivalent of feeding our dark wolf.

Mental adaptability, or having cognitive control, is the ability to switch our ways of thinking in situations that require flexibility.

Take control of your mind and mood, instead of your mind and fake news managing you.

MENTAL ADAPTABILITY RECIPE

You are a unique individual, so how you respond to even the most longed-for change will depend on a combination of factors. These include your beliefs and attitudes, past experiences, social supports, resources and security needs.

Chances are you're already adaptable when it comes to making small adjustments in your day-to-day life. And you may not even be conscious of many of your adaptations – swerving to avoid a pothole in the road; changing your takeaway order if your favourite café is closed that day; catching a bus if your train is delayed; organising for your partner to pick up the children from school when you realise your meeting will run over time.

But there are many new situations – positive and anticipated, as well as challenging and tough – that can shake our sense of self and wellbeing, where mental adaptability and resilience can help:

- getting married (or divorced)
- a major health scare or injury
- changing jobs
- adjusting to a new manager at work
- changing your exercise or nutritional habits
- moving to a new town or state
- the loss of a loved one
- a new baby (or fur baby) joining the family.

YOUR MENTAL ADAPTABILITY STARTING POINT

Spend five minutes answering the following questions to see how mentally adaptable you are right now.

How open-minded are you? How willing are you to try new ways of doing things?

How flexible are you? How do you cope with interruptions or changes in schedule?

Think about a few occasions in the past when you've had to adapt to new or changing situations. How did you respond?

What part of the change process was the easiest for you, and what part was the most difficult?

THREE KEYS FOR CULTIVATING ADAPTABILITY

No matter how you answered these questions, there are three key skills to cultivate that will support your mental adaptability:

1. **Mindfulness:** learn to manage your attention.
2. **Control:** master what you can control, and let go of what you can't.
3. **Perspective:** see the view from both the balcony and the dance floor.

Let's look at each in more detail.

1. Mindfulness

Taking a mindful approach helps you focus on the here and now rather than dwelling on the past or worrying about the future. Research shows that as the mind wanders, it easily gets trapped into patterns and negative thinking.

Mentally adaptable people are able to be present and engaged, enabling them to deal with a situation as it is rather than as they think it should be.

Research shows that mindfulness keeps you mentally, emotionally and physically happy. Mindfulness can literally rewire your brain to help you cultivate emotional intelligence and reduce stress.

I find that mindfulness tends to elicit the same reaction as coriander (cilantro): you either love it or hate it. Part of the challenge with mindfulness is that it has become almost synonymous with meditation.

I would like to frame mindfulness for you as a helpful skill – regardless of whether you are interested in meditation or not.

A very simple definition of mindfulness from Happify that I like is, 'Mindfulness is the ability to know what's happening in your head at any given moment, without getting carried away by it.'

The key elements to mindfulness are:

- noticing and becoming aware of your thoughts and emotions
- observing whatever comes up without judgement, criticism or analysis
- not becoming immersed in, attached to, overinvested in or consumed by your thoughts and emotions
- letting your thoughts and emotions go.

Mindfulness is not about:

- emptying your mind of all thoughts and emotions
- judging your thoughts as good or bad, positive or negative
- competition, challenge, success or failure.

Start where you are now.

At the height of the global financial crisis, my workaholism was peaking at 80-hour weeks, my anxiety over staff jobs was through the roof, my internal stress meter had exploded and I was yet to receive a diagnosis of burnout. A good friend suggested I try meditation.

I dragged myself off to an eight-week meditation course that ran for two hours each Thursday night. While everyone sat calmly around me, cross-legged on cushions in a dim candle-lit room, imagining their thoughts as puffy white clouds to push off into the horizon, I was bouncing off the walls. My thoughts were on steroids fuelled by stress and adrenalin, and I couldn't conjure up one single fluffy white cloud. My feelings of failure fed the overwhelm I had been experiencing before I even arrived at the course. When I left the first night (early), I was shattered.

Much later, I started taking yoga classes, which were a much better fit for where I was at. The movement of yoga helped me move the nervous energy out of my system, balancing my breathing enabled me to move out of my SNS, and the repetitious flow sequences helped focus my mind's attention and provide a sense of calm.

So, I encourage you to find a mindfulness activity that resonates for you.

Mind full or mindful?

One way of developing mindfulness is meditation, but simply spending five to ten minutes a day focusing on something that supports you to stay in the present also works.

Mindfulness practices you might like to consider include:

- focusing on your breath: inhale, exhale, focusing on breathing sensations
- paying attention to each detail of eating your food
- walking in nature and drinking in your surrounds
- sitting by the ocean, observing the ebb and flow of the water
- fishing in a river, noticing the line, ripples in the water, bubbles of air and sounds of the birds
- knitting, crafting, drawing, painting, colouring in, baking – where you become fully absorbed in the activity
- a yoga sequence where breath, mind, body and spirit come together in flow
- gardening, building, sculpting
- cycling, swimming, jogging, skiing, surfing.

The more we practise mindfulness, the better we get at it, and the more benefits we experience.

The good news is that the frequency of mindfulness practice is more important than the duration. So, spending five to ten minutes each morning and night cultivating mindfulness will be more helpful than meditating for 90 minutes once a week.

This is not to be confused with switching off or zoning out, such as watching a movie or gaming, or a relaxation activity like a guided meditation, massage, podcast or music that puts you to sleep.

Mindfulness involves slowing down, paying attention, suspending judgement and fully engaging in whatever experience is happening in the present moment.

Meditation

Mindfulness meditation has become increasingly popular. And research supports meditation as being highly effective in helping people be more mindful in their daily practices.

Meditation is a practice where an individual uses a technique – such as mindfulness or focusing the mind on a particular object, thought or activity – to train attention and awareness with the intention of achieving a mentally clear and emotionally calm and stable state. Mindfulness meditation is simply a category of meditation.

If you find a practice that works for you, the most important thing is to be patient, consistent in a routine and intentional about what you hope to cultivate within yourself.

The simplest mindfulness meditation practice for tuning in and developing your focus is to observe your breathing.

1. Find a quiet, private place to minimise external distractions.
2. Set a timer for three to five minutes so that your mind isn't tracking the time.
3. Sit in a neutral, upright, seated position to help you stay alert and free from physical discomfort and distractions.
4. Close your eyes to reduce the distractions that come with sight.

5. Gently focus your attention on your breathing. As you inhale, notice the cool temperature, the air passing through your nostrils, where in your torso you are breathing from. As you exhale, notice the warm temperature, the air passing through your nostrils and over the top of your lip.
6. If you are finding it difficult to stay focused with just your breathing, you might like to add counting. Either count the number of seconds it takes for you to inhale and then the number of seconds to exhale, or count the number of your breaths from one through to ten and then back from ten to one.
7. When you notice your mind wandering, just gently bring your attention back to your breathing, or back to counting your breaths.

The more often you practise, the greater the length of time you will be able to focus before your mind wanders off.

Breathe in, breathe out. Repeat.

If you find yourself stuck on a negative thought or harshly judging a situation, ask yourself four questions, as shown in Figure 8.

Figure 8: Thoughts are not facts

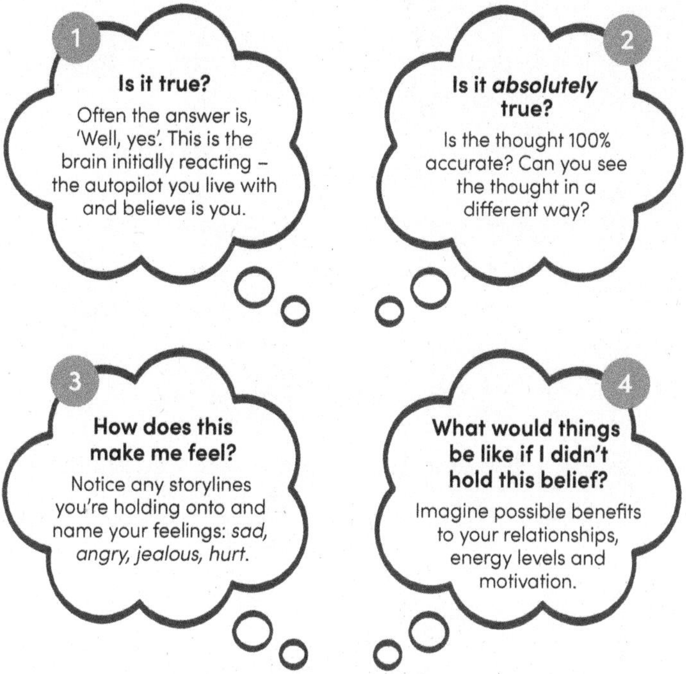

Excerpt from *Uncovering Happiness* by Elisha Goldstein, Ph.D., adapted from *Loving What Is* by Byron Katie.

Over time, you will notice that you are managing your mind more than your mind is managing you.

Just as putting space between our emotions and reactions changes our relationship with our emotional triggers, we can do a similar exercise with our thoughts. The practice of mindfulness helps us to watch our thoughts come and go instead of thinking of them as facts.

QUICK BITE

A simple and popular mindfulness practice is to combine breathing with a body scan.

1. Sit in a straight but comfortable position for five to ten minutes – close your eyes, turn your attention inward and balance the length of your inhale and exhale breaths.
2. Then, starting with the extremities (such as your toes), slowly scan each part of your body, working upwards.
3. Notice where the energy flows freely and where your body is holding tension. Don't analyse or judge; simply notice and then move on to the next part.
4. If you are finding it difficult to stay focused, you may like to mentally label and number your progress. Left big toe, second toe, third toe, fourth toe, little toe, left shin, left calf and so on.
5. When you discover your mind wandering, just gently bring your attention back to your breathing, or back to counting your breaths.

2. Control

Some challenges and decisions are beyond your control. With the external force of gravity, a stream flows down a mountain. If a fish fights this current and tries to swim upwards, it will exhaust itself and not get far. Flowing downwards brings ease and progress.

You can't change events, but you can change the way you interpret and react to them.

Particularly in high-care and low-control situations, we can become overly invested in emotional reactions and ruminative thinking that isn't helpful. And then we miss or overlook options and actions that we could take to move us forward.

We often see this cycle playing out at work. Rumours filter through that a large change or restructure may be coming. People naturally start feeling anxious in the face of ambiguity, uncertainty and incomplete information. They reach out to as many people as possible to try to find out what is going on and how it will affect them. People start creating 'facts' to fill in the blanks in the stories. Under stress, people can become distracted to the point where their ability to concentrate on their own work suffers and they may fall behind.

An important skill in mental adaptability is being able to shape your sense of control. This starts with being aware of and identifying what is within your control and what is outside of your control.

Figure 9 shows a control assessment matrix to help with this.

Figure 9: Control assessment matrix

	Areas of control	Areas of no control
Take action	Mastery	Spinning wheels
Take no action	Give up	Let go

In the rumoured restructure example, getting worked up over events that may or may not happen, with partial information that may or may not be true, fuels anxiety and is not a helpful response.

Spinning wheels

Picture your car getting bogged in quicksand. The harder you press on the accelerator, the more the wheels spin, the quicker you sink and more stuck you get.

Give up

You may give up, throw your hands in the air, leave the car to sink and allow the mud to get into the engine. You take photos of your car submerging, post them on social media and look for people to commiserate with you.

Both of these are unhelpful responses – you become consumed with rumination and helplessness and give up your power.

Let's look at the more helpful response options.

Mastery

It is important to take positive action on the things that are within your control.

So, rather than spinning your wheels, call for help, get out of the car to reduce the weight, and look for branches or wood that you can put under the wheels to slow the rate of sinking.

Let go

When situations and events are outside of your control, it is important to recognise when you don't have influence and let go. Don't overinvest your time and energy.

In the sinking car example, you may not find anything suitable to put under the wheels to stop it sinking. Rather than jumping on social media and distressing yourself further, you could spend your waiting time calling the insurance company to get the claim for financial and repair support started.

You control how you respond.

When facing ambiguity and uncertainty, it helps to take stock of what control you have in the situation. What choices can you make? What pathways could you take, given different possible outcomes?

In the rumoured restructure example, unless you are the CEO or Head of HR, you don't have direct control over the what, where, when or how of the impending event. So, it is important that you tap into the networks that are most likely to know the facts first, and then let go of the excess noise.

Managing your reaction, performing your job, investing in your relationships with key stakeholders and preparing broadly and well for alternative career paths and work options are all within your control.

It is helpful to invest your time and energy into putting your best foot forward when change starts to roll through.

Your turn.

Writing out your thoughts exercise

Doing a brain dump and getting your thoughts out of your head by writing them down reduces their potency. Worrying takes up cognitive resources. Research shows that if we unload our worries, it frees up more space in our brains to think of other things and work towards the tasks we are completing. And it promotes greater flexibility.

It's kind of like people who struggle with worry are constantly multitasking – they are doing one task and trying to monitor and suppress their worries at the same time.

Writing down your thoughts not only helps to 'get them out of your head', but it also allows you to view them more rationally.

Try it out for yourself.

Think of a recent event that you have been struggling with that has become an earworm for you. You can't get it out of your head, no matter how hard you try.

Try writing it down.

1. Write down the thought or thoughts that are stuck in your head – write free flow, without editing.

2. Write down some options on what could help offset the thoughts.

3. Note the things that are out of your control with regard to the thoughts.

4. Note the things that you do have control over in relation to the thoughts.

5. Take a moment to reflect on how you are feeling in relation to your thoughts at the end of this exercise. What has changed?

QUICK BITE

Here are some tips for reducing the potency of unhelpful thoughts:

- Move: change up your physiology.
- Make a plan and take an action towards resolving unresolved issues that are taking up mental space.
- Talk it through with a friend and gain another perspective.

3. Perspective

The Buddha once asked a student: 'If a person is struck by an arrow, is it painful? If the person is struck by a second arrow, is it even more painful?'

He then went on to explain, 'In life, we cannot always control the first arrow. However, the second arrow is our reaction to the first. And with this second arrow comes the possibility of choice.'

These second arrows, our emotional and mental responses to situations and crises, are natural and human. But the truth is that they can often bring us more suffering by narrowing and cluttering our mind and keeping us from clearly seeing the best course of action.

Developing our perspective-taking capacity builds our resilience and opens up our mental and creative pathways. It buffers our wellbeing in the face of adversity and challenge.

**When you change the way you see things,
the things you see start to change.**

We each have a uniquely valuable perspective on life, a lens through which we interpret our lives. Through our perspective, we define what makes sense to us, which is differentiated from how others see and experience life.

Say my manager tells me I haven't done a good job on a piece of work. My emotional and mental response won't just be to that event; it will relate to all the other experiences I have had that my mind tells me are similar – conversations with this manager, with previous managers, with other colleagues and possibly even that time 30 years ago in Year 4 when my teacher shouted at me.

It will also be influenced by what I have learnt from family, friends and school. This could include my brother telling me that most managers are idiots, the theory I learnt about how high-performing managers should deliver feedback, along with my own childhood belief that I am not good enough. The internal factors – beliefs, experiences, opinions – influencing my response will be numerous. But they are only a small part of the picture.

In this example, it would be easy to become enmeshed in a defensive, reactive position with my manager. When your mind gets stuck, a chain reaction begins. Fear begins to narrow your field of vision, and it becomes harder to see the bigger picture and the positive, creative possibilities in front of you. As perspective shrinks, so too does your ability to connect with others and find a constructive way forward.

We don't know what we don't know, and perspective-taking provides a powerful tool to expand our own perspective by learning from the way others see life.

Instead of getting defensive and narrowing our options, perspective-taking allows for growth and fostering options. It is the equivalent of seeing life through a tunnel and then having someone break down the sides of the tunnel to create a more expansive perspective on life. Multiple perspectives are crucial to gain a full understanding of a concept, situation, experience or environment.

If your manager's feedback and behaviour doesn't make sense to you, it is most likely because you don't have enough information. What does a 'good job' mean to your manager? How does this differ to your interpretation of a good job? What is the intent behind their critical feedback? To help you learn? Grow? Develop? Improve? Fill a skill gap? What do they need you to change or do differently to improve?

Looking through a lens of curiosity and real interest in understanding the other person and their behaviour opens perspective rather than closing it.

Perspective-taking is a core resilience skill that helps you navigate your way through choppy water. It is the ability to look beyond your own point of view so that you can consider how someone else may think or feel about something.

It allows you to see beyond your choppy water and make out a boat, a lighthouse, deadly rocks, land, or the sun rising up over the horizon.

Three key strategies to broaden your perspective

To help broaden your perspective, use one of these three strategies.

1. **Foster positive emotions.** We have learnt that positive emotions widen a person's outlook in small ways that, over time, can reshape who they are. Joy, for example, creates the urge to play, push the limits and be creative.

**Avoid black-and-white thinking.
Rather than making something right or wrong
and getting caught in judgement labels,
look for the interesting shades of grey.**

2. **Approach with curiosity.** One of my favourite mindset tactics comes from Celeste Headlee, a talk show host in the USA who did a fabulous TED Talk on how to have better conversations. 'Everyone knows something that you don't know. Approach every conversation prepared to be amazed.' How could you not broaden your perspective with such an open and interested mind?
3. **Develop empathy.** Imagine the world from another person's shoes – and then another, and another. Look for balance. Draw up a list of pros and cons, and look for additional information to contribute to the shorter side of the list.

**Developing this kind of mental adaptability
will help you distinguish between what is important
and what is noise, and helps you calmly deal with
uncertainty, challenge and change.**

QUICK BITE

Stuck in a rut?

Physical exercise increases your energy levels, shifts perspective, reduces your worries and can distract you from the repetitive thinking patterns that get stuck in your head.

Just 20 minutes of intensive exercise causes your brain to release dopamine, serotonin, opioids, endorphins, neurotrophics and endocannabinoids – feel-good chemicals that allow the body and brain to learn and grow. Over time, exercise stabilises mood, increases the size of the hippocampus and promotes neurogenesis. All of these things enhance cognitive flexibility.

RESILIENCE RECIPE #4

FROM SILO TO SUCCESS

Jennifer was a mid-level manager at a well-regarded professional services firm. She was known for her strong work ethic and great attention to detail, and as someone who could be relied upon to go the extra mile to over-deliver to clients. She loved to learn, had a strength in process improvement and was driven and ambitious.

At each performance review, she would present her list of achievements for the previous six months and ask for the pathway and timeline for promotion. Every time she was told that she was a technical specialist who had reached her promotional ceiling. The clear message was that she needed to improve her interpersonal skills across the business and people-development skills within her team.

Jennifer doubled down and worked harder. She took on more of her department's workload and contributed to more process-improvement projects. She believed this was more than enough for her to be recognised and promoted.

When we started mentoring, our starting point was to seek others' perspectives and redefine Jennifer's understanding of the criteria for promotion. Jennifer's first learning exercise was to seek feedback on her strengths and weakness from a range of stakeholders across the business. It turned out her direct reports experienced her as cold and unapproachable. Her department leaders found her dogmatic and inflexible. The partners on the talent committee said she lacked visibility and contribution to the overall business.

Jennifer was shocked by the complete mismatch between how others perceived her and her view of herself, and by the importance of seeking out a range of feedback to improve her perspective-taking. She realised that by not taking on board others' feedback, she had built an impenetrable silo around herself that, while it made her feel safe, meant promotion was all but impossible.

We put in place a development plan that focused on what was within Jennifer's control. She started by changing the way she interacted with people to improve warmth and trust. This included taking the time to get to know her team on a personal level, and showing her leaders that she was willing to try new ideas and engage in others' preferred ways of working. She instigated regular updates with the talent committee to share what she was doing and changing because of their feedback and guidance. Jennifer focused on growing her people-development skills, political savvy and stakeholder engagement. She let go of her tendency to dig in deeper when challenged and released some of her micro-management perfectionist ways of working that had been holding her back.

With a willingness to change, applied effort and embracing a broader definition of success, Jennifer was promoted to Director 18 months later. She gained a reputation for being a team player who consistently delivered results and acted in the best interests of the business. She achieved a promotion to Partner two years after that.

What mental silos do you have that are keeping you trapped? In what ways could you improve your mental adaptability and approach to life?

CHAPTER 5

OPTIMISING ENERGY

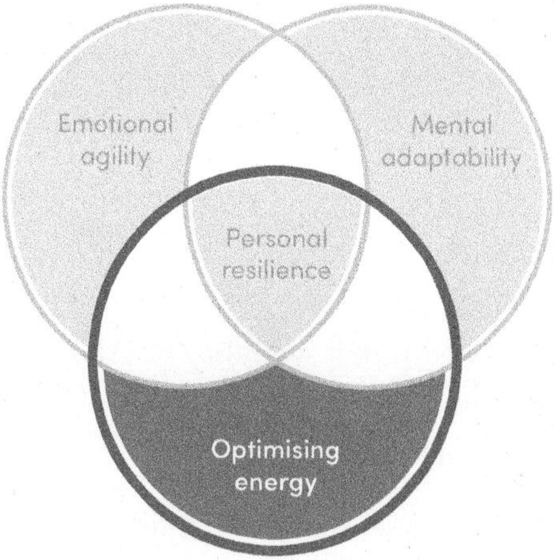

Arianna Huffington was at her desk checking email and making work calls when she collapsed. She passed out and woke up in a pool of blood with a broken cheekbone. Her default belief that led to this event was that burnout was the price of success – for being great at business and a great mum.

It wasn't until she quit her working-around-the-clock habit, prioritised sleep and implemented daily self-care that success followed. Arianna is now the founder and CEO of Thrive Global, bestselling author of *Thrive* and *The Sleep Revolution*, and is on the Forbes list of the World's 100 Most Powerful Women in 2018 and the inaugural 50 over 50 list.

> *'I can tell you with authority that when I'm exhausted, when I'm running on empty, I'm the worst version of myself.' – Arianna Huffington*

GO FOR GOLD

Much of what we read about resilience, and resilience skills, is about coping with pressure and managing adversity. Managing and sustaining our energy usually gets overlooked, yet this is critical.

When I was leading a textile company through the global financial crisis and experienced the crippling burnout that shut down my mental and physical health, my skills in dealing with pressure, managing challenge and finding pathways through adversity were in peak form.

Work always came first – before my fitness, family and friends. Breakfast, lunch and dinner were spent at my desk. But without taking the time to rest and recharge, I was working from an energy deficit that eventually gave out. And it took me two years to recover the health that I had destroyed.

We need energy to last the distance, to enable us to do everything that is important in our lives, to perform well and be at our best. Yet too often we let external influences and the environment determine or derail our priorities. Working back late on a once-off project to finish a report becomes a pattern of working back late. Forgoing personal exercise time to ferry the kids to sport becomes a pattern of deprioritising our fitness. And so on.

Think of energy as the tank of fuel that keeps you going, or the battery that keeps you charged and performing. When your energy becomes drained, motivation becomes sluggish, and it is harder to get things done.

Most of us know that the foundations of our physical health and wellbeing include regular movement, nourishing nutrition and nurturing sleep. However, too often we let 'life' get in the way of living with wellbeing. We get bogged down in the minutiae of the sand and pebbles rather than taking care of our big rocks first.

If you keep drawing on your energy without refuelling or recharging, your system will keep slowing down until you eventually come to a stop.

Optimising energy is about ensuring balanced support and investment across our emotional, mental and physical health.

Our emotions affect our nervous system, which also influences – and is influenced by – our major organs and immune defences. Work-related stress is a major contributor to elevated blood pressure and cortisol. Job strain is the greatest risk factor for heart diseases.

We also know that the effects of stress aren't just mental. Stress is also physical and affects three systems in the body:

1. hormonal
2. immune
3. digestive.

And research now shows that loneliness has one of the greatest negative impacts on our immune system defences.

There is a fine line between balance and burnout.

BALANCED OR BURNT OUT?

It's not possible to drive around with an empty tank for more than a few kilometres. If your wiper fluid isn't filled, you're in trouble when rain smears the windscreen. Tyres need the right amount of air to provide a smooth ride. Oil changes must be performed regularly to keep your car running and dependable. Even when you take good care of your car, parts wear out and emergencies still occur.

Many of us are feeling exhausted by overwork, constant connectivity and continual distractions. And we are not completing the self-care maintenance needed to sustain our energy and wellbeing.

> *'I'm not saying that you can't succeed by burning out. But you can succeed much more effectively, and much more sustainably, and with much less damage to your health and your relationships.' – Arianna Huffington*

Burnout has recently been classified as an occupational disease by the World Health Organization. The primary cause is chronic work stress, and it severely impacts our wellbeing. Burnout is typically a combination of three symptoms:

1. feelings of energy depletion and exhaustion
2. increased feelings of negativity or mental distance from your job
3. reduced functioning and efficacy.

To recover from burnout, it helps to identify which one of these symptoms is most significant and to focus action on that first. For example, with exhaustion, focus on self-care. For detachment, a focus on reconnecting with others helps. And you can bolster effectiveness by accomplishing small tasks.

However, the best cure for burnout is prevention: to protect your energy from becoming depleted in the first place.

Burnout is not an acceptable price to pay for success.

FLIP THE EQUATION

Optimal energy means having the energy to do what you want to do, to complete the things that are important to you and to do them when you want to do them. It means not burning time and energy in busyness, urgency and distractions, and neglecting the important things.

But many of us approach our energy like a time equation. We start with the tasks that need to be done, rather than investing our time and energy into the things we care about.

Shawn Achor, a former Harvard University professor and TEDx speaker, advocates flipping the equation. If we keep pushing our happiness to the other side of busyness, we will never reach it. When we strive for a promotion, a better salary or a bigger house, and promise ourselves that we will be happy when we get there, we are letting ourselves down because mentally we keep shifting the goal posts. Got a good car? Now you need a better car. Got a good job? Now you need a bigger promotion. Got a nice house? Now you need a nice house in a better neighbourhood.

So, we need to flip the equation.

Research shows that if we prioritise our wellbeing first, we become more creative, innovative and productive as a result. In real life, this looks like investing our energy into our wellbeing priorities and values first, then streamlining, automating or delegating the busy tasks that drain our energy for little return.

Manage your energy rather than your time.

SIMPLE, RIGHT?

Sounds simple, right? So, why aren't we doing it? The pushback I usually get at this point is, 'I know all this stuff already.' But the reality is that 90% of the time, when people in my workshops do this exercise, they realise that while they know what they should be doing, they aren't actually doing it.

So, stay with me here; take five minutes to work through the exercise on the next page, and make one tiny change that will shift the dial away from exhaustion and towards energy.

FIVE STEPS TO OPTIMISE YOUR ENERGY

Energy, not time, is your fundamental source of efficiency and performance.

So, optimising energy is about prioritising and protecting what fuels your wellbeing.

Step 1: Commit to your wellbeing priorities from chapter 1

Refer back to your wellbeing priorities on page 23.

Write your definition of wellbeing with any reflections, notes or adjustments:

(My definition of wellbeing is 'feeling good, functioning well, living with purpose, having fun and positively contributing'.)

Choose your three most important domains of wellbeing for your life right now:

(Examples include: fitness, family, finances, meaningful work, hobbies.)

1.

2.

3.

Step 2: Nominate your wellbeing focus and energy level from chapter 2

What does your wellbeing hourglass look like? Well resourced, or depleted?

Write your resilience wellbeing focus level with any reflections, notes or adjustments:

(Wellbeing levels: Burnout, Stuck, Functioning, Productive, Thriving.)

Now review how much energy you are generating for your three most important domains of wellbeing.

What is the gap? Where are your gaps?

Energy examples could include:

- **Physical energy:** food, water, sleep, incidental exercise
- **Emotional energy:** positive emotions from things we enjoy and find relaxing
- **Mental energy:** realistic, optimistic thinking patterns
- **Social energy:** spending quality time with family and close friends
- **Spiritual energy:** aligning with purpose, passion, values, altruism.

> Rate on a scale from 1 to 5 how much energy you are generating for each of your three important wellbeing domains, and note both your strengths and your gaps:
>
> ○—○—○—○—○
>
> 1 2 4 4 5
>
> 1 = energy drain; 3 = energy neutral; 5 = strong energy boost.

Staying on your wellbeing wagon

You also need to plan for and support success.

Many people stop at this point. And then they wonder why shortly afterwards they have trouble staying on their wellbeing wagon. We also need to plan for and support success.

The remaining three steps relate to the three key resilience skills that will help you to optimise your energy and encourage sustainable success.

These are:

1. **Boundary management** – putting boundaries around what is important, and making decisions about what you will and won't do.
2. **Healthy habit stacking** – healthy habits that make the energising things you want to achieve easy.
3. **Helpful routines and support systems** – streamlining and removing the things from your life that are causing you friction and aggravation.

Let's look at each in more detail.

Step 3: Boundary management

Envisage a school located by a busy road. During playtime, the children need to stay near the building to keep safe. The teachers need to be hypervigilant and constantly patrolling.

However, if a boundary fence is erected around the playground, the children will be free and have more space to run, play and enjoy their break time more. Teachers can roster supervision and rotate to enable rest and replenishment.

Trying to do everything often means doing nothing very well.

Trying to do too much? You have a finite amount of energy and time each day, so you need to balance it between the things that matter.

Focus your effort on driving through your priorities. Use your priorities to stay focused. Priorities act like your guiding compass when you're faced with conflicting demands. They help you maintain perspective in terms of what must be done. Take time to choose your priorities and make sure they are right for you.

Boundary management involves making choices and being deliberate about the trade-offs. It means being specific about what you will do, and also being specific about what you won't do.

This is about what you need to do to implement a boundary that will make a positive difference for you. Be deliberate. What are your non-negotiables? What will you be flexible with?

For example, I ferociously protect the first three hours of my morning. I will not hold meetings or run workshops before 10 am. Between 7 am and 10 am, I take a walk in the fresh air, meditate, do my creative work and choose my priorities for the day.

However, after 10 am I will be flexible with scheduling to accommodate my clients' needs. My personal preference is to structure my day with deep-thinking work in the mornings, and social interactive meetings and training workshops in the afternoons. This supports the ebb and flow of my circadian rhythm and optimal energy times.

Now it is your turn.

How will you set up your day for success?

How would your ideal working day be structured?

What will you start, stop or maintain to boost your energy?

Start:

Stop:

Maintain:

Now apply this thinking to your wellbeing priorities.

What will you start, stop or maintain to support your wellbeing priorities?

Start:

Stop: ______________________________

____

____

____

Maintain: ______________________________

____

____

____

QUICK BITE

Making a small number of key boundary decisions well is more important than making a large number of decisions.

If you short-change your sleep, you might get a couple of extra work hours, but are those two hours productive?

Are you overinvesting in social media conversations that drain energy at the expense of investing in quality time with friends and family that boosts your social wellbeing?

Let's now look at how we can be more successful in implementing our wellbeing priorities, and how healthy habit stacking makes sticking to your priorities easier.

Step 4: Healthy habit stacking

We don't just wake up one morning, jump out of bed and climb Mt Everest. It takes planning, preparation, training and practice runs on smaller climbs to develop the energy, fitness and stamina required.

Most mountain paths are not direct routes to the summit but take us up and down through valleys, fields and rivers to lead us to the next peak. And as we hike each section of the track, we experience new viewpoints. Different perspectives are revealed and we stop regularly to pause, rest and recharge.

It takes work, determination and sometimes sheer perseverance to get where we wish to go. An important part of resilience is maintaining personal energy, which we need to recharge and replenish. Taking adequate time out to recover and rejuvenate is key for a productive and fulfilling life.

Healthy basics

When it comes to the basics of health, most of us acknowledge the go-to categories as being what we eat, how we move and getting sufficient sleep. Tom Rath's informative and engaging book *Eat Move Sleep* shows how tiny healthy choices in these areas lead to larger positive changes.

But I invite you to think of optimising energy as being about more than just physical health. Look more broadly and include the wellbeing domains of emotional, mental, social and spiritual health. Climbing our personal mountains also requires motivation, goal striving, mental focus, social support and so forth.

There are four healthy habit stacking categories to plan around:

1. **Rest:** sleep, breaks, relaxation, listening to music, mindfulness, breathing
2. **Recharge:** play, hobbies, social connection, time in nature, gratitude

3. **Fitness:** movement, exercise, mobility, flexibility, strength, stamina
4. **Fuel:** nutrition, hydration, energy.

I like to think of work and rest as the yin and yang of happiness. Both are complementary and opposing forces.

Work drives wellbeing in areas such as purpose, achievement, finances and contribution. Rest includes wellbeing sources such as relaxation, breaks and flow-inducing activities. Both are necessary conditions for appreciating the other. And the interplay of energy can be considered most powerful when they are in balance.

I invite you to take five minutes and brainstorm what your healthy basics will include.

As you do this exercise, refer to your wellbeing priorities. And make sure you cover the categories of rest, recharge, fitness and fuel.

Healthy habits

Put simply, healthy habits are habits that are good for you mentally, physically and socially. They include short-term incentives and built-in support, and provide a long-term pay-off.

For example, 15 minutes of morning meditation provides clarity and focus for the day, supports emotional and mental wellbeing and, with regular practice, improves the quality of your sleep.

Another example of a healthy habit is a regular weekly walk in the park with a good friend. It provides social connection, physical exercise that builds fitness and a wellbeing boost from spending time in nature.

What are your current healthy habits?

What healthy habits would you like to build to support one of your wellbeing strengths or cover a wellbeing gap?

QUICK BITE

Try the 20/20/20 formula from Robin Sharma's book *The 5am Club*. Start your morning with 20 minutes to move and sweat, 20 minutes to reflect and 20 minutes to grow (for example, through reading).

Habit stacking

Whether you realise it or not, many of the actions you take throughout the day are done out of habit. This includes things like brushing your teeth, checking your phone first thing in the morning or watching the 6 pm news.

Habit stacking is pretty much exactly what it sounds like. It's about creating new, healthy habits by stacking them on top of habits you already have.

James Clear is one of the more well-known habit experts. He explains that because your current habits are already ingrained into your brain, it's easier to use them to create new habits. By linking your new habits to existing habits, they're more likely to stick. And when you've mastered one habit, you can continue to stack on new habits.

Create new healthy habits by stacking them on top of habits you already have.

Think about your morning routine. It's essentially just a bunch of habits stacked on top of one another.

Choose a trigger that happens every single morning. Then set your intention for a new habit you want to do and link it to your chosen trigger.

It will look like, 'After I do this, I will do that.' For example:

- After I turn my alarm off in the morning, I will drink a glass of water.
- After I get out of bed, I will go for a walk around the park.
- After I have my coffee, I will spend five minutes meditating and savouring the silence.
- After I brush my teeth, I will do ten minutes of stretches.

Once you've created a new, consistent habit using the habit-stacking method, you can start adding more habits. When you do this, you're creating a habit staircase.

Here are some tips for creating your habit staircase:

- Start small. If you start by trying to add a 30-minute habit on the first day, you may not be able to sustain it. Whatever habit it is you're trying to add, start with just five minutes and build up.
- Create a reminder for yourself that you will see every single day. This could be your morning alarm message, a Post-it Note on the coffee machine or your exercise clothes laid out at the end of your bed.
- Track your habit, and make it satisfying by ticking off your progress.
- Wait until you've mastered one habit before adding another to the stack.

Here is an example of a habit staircase morning routine:

- Alarm goes off, drink the glass of water by the bed.
- See your set-out exercise clothes, put them on and head out for a walk.
- Return from your walk, make a coffee.
- Sit quietly with the coffee and meditate for five minutes.
- Shower and get ready for work.

Bookend your day with a winding-down habit stack.

An evening routine is the perfect time to build in relaxation and resting habits. Here are some starting ideas to consider for an evening habit stack:

- Spending three minutes reflecting on your day with gratitude.
- Connecting with the family over a board game.
- Decompressing with 15 minutes of reading a fiction book.
- Taking a mineral salts bath.
- Doing ten minutes of yoga stretches.
- Taking a five-minute guided visual meditation that promotes sleep.

Your turn.

Take one of your identified healthy habits and add it to one of your automatic morning habits.

Now take one of your identified healthy habits and add it to an automatic evening habit.

QUICK BITE

Here are some tips for loving your morning routine:

- Start your morning with something you love to jump out of bed early for.
- Focus on energising activities.
- Set a positive intention for your day that you focus on during your morning routine.
- Give yourself time in the morning for your best work, before other tasks.

Let's now look at how we can make sure we have the space and energy to maintain our healthy habit stacking.

Step 5: Helpful routines and support systems

Hitting the snooze button on your alarm is actually a waste of your precious energy. This may seem counterintuitive, but half slumbering is like revving a car without putting it into gear. Both activities waste fuel.

Think of your willpower as a muscle. It tires with use, and it depletes over time. But it can also be strengthened with exercise.

Decision fatigue is a depletion of energy that makes it difficult for us to resist distractions and temptations. But we can design our environment to energise rather than exhaust us.

Making simple changes to our practices through helpful routines can help us to optimise and recharge our energy, to achieve our full potential without exhausting our willpower and energy.

Think of this as a system for streamlining and removing the things from your life that are causing you friction and aggravation.

Helpful routines switch us out of effort and into ease. The daily wardrobe of Mark Zuckerberg, the founder of Facebook, consists of a grey T-shirt and blue jeans. He made his clothing choice once and now doesn't waste his daily energy on what he considers to be low-value clothing choices.

Switching from effort to ease is about:

- reducing the overload of daily decisions
- automating, delegating or outsourcing low-value tasks.

Think of helpful routines like a fish swimming downstream. It is taking advantage of the existing flow and momentum of its environment, rather than battling against the natural tide and exhausting itself for little return by heading upstream.

Examples of helpful routines include:

- batch-cooking on one night to create meals for the week ahead, or cooking double portions of dinner to provide lunch for the next day
- setting your alarm to get out of bed the same time every day
- laying out your exercise clothes the night before
- starting each day with a protein-packed smoothie
- setting up direct debits for bill payments.

Set yourself up for success with helpful routines and support systems:

- Plan your day ahead to protect your priorities and avoid overwhelm. Block out time in your calendar, not just for meetings but to ensure you have time to do important work, take a lunch break and exercise.
- Be realistic about your expectations and standards. Think in terms of 'good enough' rather than guilt.
- Get help from others:
  - Invest in a cleaner once a fortnight, or once a month.
  - Outsource the ironing of your business shirts.
  - Have a professional do your tax.
  - Share school drop-offs and pick-ups with neighbours.
  - Pay the kids to do weekly chores that benefit the whole household.

Brainstorm a list of all the things that you can think of that are a daily drain on your energy:

Take the top three energy drainers from your list and choose a way to automate, delegate or outsource them:

WHERE TO NEXT?

Much of the stuff in this chapter feels basic, like going back to preschool, but we aren't doing it. This is why you need to periodically revisit how you are spending your time each day and recalibrate when you slip out of balance.

Make your unconscious time-wasters conscious, and actively choose. Choose your balance and create boundaries, rather than staying stuck on the same busyness treadmill.

Create the space and routines that will optimise your energy, time and resources to do what is important for you and your wellbeing.

QUICK BITE

Here are some simple daily changes to help recharge energy at work:

- Carve out time for deep work at the time of day when you are at your best. Schedule administrative tasks for lulls and meetings for when your energy is flagging.
- Turn off message and email notifications on your phone and computer. When the notification ping or banner goes off, it's really hard to resist the urge to check your messages immediately. So, why not remove the temptation altogether and only check your inbox at designated times?
- Have a lunch break, preferably with your colleagues. Don't skip lunch – and don't eat alone – if you can help it. Not only does skipping lunch deplete your energy that same day, but research suggests it can also interfere with your sleep and exhaustion over the weekend. And when we share lunch with other people, the social interaction releases feel-good endorphins into the brain.
- Go for a walk. Studies from researchers at Stanford University have found that walks help boost both our creativity and our concentration. Add a social and professional element to them by having a walking meeting with a colleague.

RESILIENCE RECIPE #5

PERMISSION TO CARE

The management group of a large, successful construction-industry company was experiencing high stress, exhaustion and change fatigue. Over three years, it had successfully delivered sales and profit growth while also bringing together three separate business units into one division and consolidating 13 sites into 8. Morale was falling, the number of safety issues was rising and good people were leaving.

The leadership team identified that the pace of transition wasn't sustainable without investing back into their people by developing resilience-building skills and creating a culture of wellbeing.

I launched a 12-month program with a carefully crafted one-day workshop of learning, fun, opportunities to connect, group discussion, reflection on personal wellbeing, and skills support for stress management and resilience.

Feedback from the management group at the lunch break was that the workshop was enjoyable and that they had gained helpful new ideas and strategies to better manage stress... But! While wellbeing was important, why were we talking about it at work? Wasn't wellbeing something that you figured out and fixed in your own time at home? Wouldn't the training day be better spent working out how to deliver the sales budget and resolve the stock issues?

I opened the afternoon session by sharing the research on why it was a smart business practice to prioritise wellbeing as a tool to better performance, and the role wellbeing plays in boosting sales, customer service, innovation and problem-solving. The flood gates opened. The increase in energy in the room was palpable. Ideas and conversations flowed. The group reorganised themselves to work in small break-out groups to come up with different ways to support better wellbeing for each other and their teams.

By the end of the day, the group had a range of activities that they agreed to help each other with. This included things such as:

- covering work to enable colleagues to leave early to attend school concerts
- commitments to support each other to join sports teams, and prioritising making it to weeknight training sessions
- agreeing not to hold meetings at lunchtime
- pushing back 8 am team meetings to 9 am to better accommodate those with young children.

I asked what had changed between the morning and afternoon sessions. By sharing the business case for wellbeing, I had given them permission to care. They now had the psychological safety to share what was important to them, to set personal and professional boundaries and be supported by their peers to action new healthy activities.

Following the 12-month focus on improving safety and wellbeing, the company scorecard showed increases in resilience, team cohesion and engagement, with significant reductions in sick leave, injuries and staff turnover.

Have you given yourself permission to prioritise your wellbeing? Are you protecting your health and fitness as non-negotiables? Or do your boundaries need repairing and reinforcement?

PART III

ENJOYING THE MEAL

THE PANTRY STAPLES of eggs, butter and milk can transform into a range of culinary creations that are more than just meal options.

A tasty, savoury omelette to kickstart the day. A nourishing frittata packed with protein and vitamins. Fluffy pancakes for a sweet treat. A sumptuous sponge cake for celebrating.

Combining our core resilience ingredients gives us superfood combinations. These transform our wellbeing recipes to punch well above their weight.

Hence, combining our three resilience ingredients will give us three boosters that can help us to move through life with wellbeing, as shown in Figure 10.

Figure 10: Three wellbeing boosters

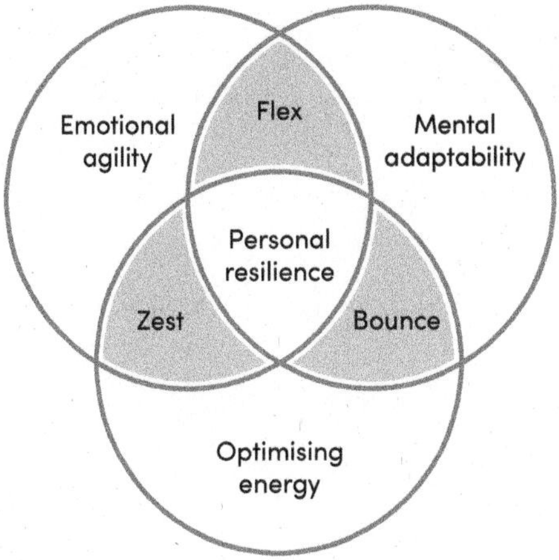

The three ingredients are:

1. **Flex:** Developing both emotional agility and mental adaptability skills helps us to flow and flex rather than break in the face of pressure, uncertainty and change.
2. **Bounce:** Combining the skills of mental adaptability with managing energy helps us to bounce forward through challenges and bounce back when adversity knocks us down.
3. **Zest:** Building both emotional agility and optimising our energy provides a resilience springboard for us to live our best life with vitality and flow.

Resilience supercharges your way to better wellbeing. Let's look at each of our three boosters in turn.

CHAPTER 6

FLEX, BOUNCE AND ZEST

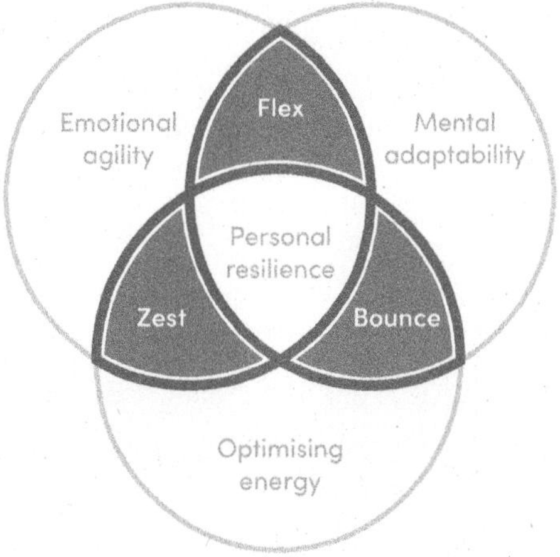

Remember the tree from chapter 2? Despite existing in a harsh climate, it consistently reaches for the sky. It grows faster and stronger when nourished with the optimal blend of sunlight, rain and nutrient-rich soil. In a storm, it flows with the weather conditions rather than resisting, and during drought it focuses on preservation and survival.

This is exactly what it means to be resilient.

Developing our emotional agility and mental adaptability helps us to flex and flow rather than bruise and break in the face of pressure, uncertainty and change. We need to understand that how we respond to challenges determines how they affect us – not the events themselves. Optimal energy and emotional agility support us with the zest to live our best life and roll over the bumps in the road. Here's how I think of the three boosters:

1. **Flex** – Being able to bend, flex and flow through uncertainty, stress, pressure and change.
2. **Bounce** – Moving through tough challenges and adversity with compassion, growth, and optimism – bouncing back and bouncing forward.
3. **Zest** – Creating the energy and vitality to live your best life and roll through the bumps and blocks in the road.

Let's look at each of these in more detail.

LEARNING TO FLEX

Resilient people learn from their mistakes rather than deny them. They see obstacles as challenges rather than roadblocks, and they allow adversity to shape them and make them stronger rather than falling down and staying down.

They look for meaning and learning in life's challenges rather than seeing themselves as victims. All these attributes bolster and fuel wellbeing.

Two helpful skill sets that support this flexibility aspect of resilience are emotional intelligence and compassion. Both are developed by deepening our self-awareness.

Developing emotional intelligence

Emotional intelligence, or EQ, is the ability to have self-awareness and self-manage your emotions, combined with the skill to accurately recognise, identify, assess and interpret the emotions of others.

Developing emotional intelligence involves developing your awareness of how you show up when you are triggered, and how this impacts your relationships with yourself, others and the world around you.

Research shows that people with high emotional intelligence are generally more successful in life. They know how to proportionately respond to change and challenge, are aware of their strengths and weaknesses, are empathetic to themselves and others, and focus on the positives. They're not worried about perfection or unnecessarily burning energy dwelling on past mistakes.

Whether they're working towards outward goals or on inner coping strategies, they're action-oriented – they trust in the process and themselves and don't give up. They are more likely to keep working towards a goal when they are faced with an obstacle. They don't feel helpless or hopeless when they are facing a challenge.

I work with a lot of people in customer-service roles, for example, who are often on the receiving end of angry calls from people who have reached the end of their tether with something that has not met their expectations. They often pick up the phone and experience an outpouring of negative feelings such as frustration, anger, distress or sadness.

Without emotional intelligence, it would be easy to absorb the stream of negativity, let it trigger their own stress response, take what is said as a personal attack and react to the perceived injustice and threat to their sense of self.

People with emotional awareness understand what they are feeling and why. They are also more likely to recognise and understand others' feelings better because they are more in touch with their own.

This type of emotional understanding enables greater flexibility, choice and control. It allows people to respond appropriately to others, and to better regulate and cope with difficult emotions such as anger or fear.

There are four aspects to emotional intelligence:

1. self-awareness
2. social awareness
3. self-management
4. relationship management.

Some of the resilience skill sets that contribute to our overall emotional intelligence are shown in Figure 11.

Figure 11: Emotional intelligence skills

Self-awareness • Emotional awareness • Accurate self-assessment • Self-compassion • Self-confidence	**Social awareness** • Accuracy of assessing others' emotions • Empathy • Service orientation
Self-management • Self-regulation • Adaptability • Optimism • Growth mindset	**Relationship management** • Inspiring • Influencing • Developing others • Conflict management

Developing compassion

Things will not always go the way you want them to. You will encounter frustrations; losses will occur; you will make mistakes, bump up against your limitations and fall short of your expectations. This is a reality shared by all of us. The more you allow this reality instead of constantly fighting against it, the more compassion you will feel for yourself and others.

Compassion is the feeling that arises when you are confronted with another's suffering and feel motivated to relieve that suffering. When this occurs, you feel warmth, caring and the desire to help the suffering person in some way. Having compassion also means that you offer understanding and kindness to others when they fail or make mistakes, rather than judging them harshly.

Resilience is based on compassion for ourselves as well as compassion for others.

Research has shown that when we feel compassion, our heart rate slows down, we secrete the 'bonding hormone' oxytocin, and regions of the brain linked to empathy, caregiving and feelings of pleasure light up. So, compassion is good for health and wellbeing.

Taking this a step further, self-compassion involves acting the same way towards yourself when you are having a difficult time, fail, or notice something you don't like about yourself. Instead of just ignoring your pain with a 'stiff upper lip' mentality, you stop and acknowledge, 'This is really difficult right now. How can I comfort and care for myself in this moment?'

Instead of judging and criticising yourself for inadequacies and shortcomings, self-compassion means you are kind and understanding when confronted with personal failings.

It is about being warm and understanding towards ourselves when we suffer, fail or feel inadequate, rather than ignoring our pain or beating ourselves up with self-criticism.

Self-compassionate people recognise that being imperfect, failing and experiencing life's difficulties is inevitable, so they tend to be gentle with themselves when confronted with painful experiences rather than getting angry when life falls short of set ideals.

Fighting against suffering increases stress, frustration and self-criticism. When we accept reality with sympathy and kindness, we experience greater emotional equanimity or balance. Self-compassion can activate our parasympathetic nervous system (PNS), which calms our fight-or-flight response.

Being compassionate to yourself means being happy and healthy in the long term. It is not to be mistaken with self-indulgence – self-indulgence is different to self-compassion. Taking a day off from healthy eating is different to creating a habit of overeating or being a couch potato, which will harm your wellbeing over time.

Cultivating self-compassion

Self-compassion involves directing feelings of kindness and care towards ourselves, and focusing our attention and energy on how we might alleviate our pain.

Choose to love yourself exactly as you are.
Know that you are a work in progress.
Be compassionate about the things you would like to change. Every evening, choose to forgive yourself.
You did the best you could.

By practising ways to support the PNS, we can cultivate an attitude of kindness, warmth, concern, understanding and strength within ourselves, and then use this attitude to respond to our struggles, rather than reverting to our usual self-critical habits.

Your turn. How is your self-compassion?

We are often our own harshest critics. The same things we berate ourselves for, we show kindness and understanding to our friends for. What would change if you responded to yourself in the same way you respond to a close friend when they are suffering?

The more we practise being kind and compassionate with ourselves, the more we'll increase the habit of self-compassion. What small self-care practices can you build into your daily routine?

QUICK BITE

Here are five tips for cultivating self-compassion:

1. Practise slow breathing to kickstart the PNS.
2. Practise mindfulness as a way to centre yourself in the moment.
3. Let yourself make mistakes.
4. Reframe automatic critical self-talk: 'It's okay that I feel upset'; 'It's human to make mistakes.'
5. Let go of the need for external validation. Don't tie your happiness to others' expectations.

BEGINNING TO BOUNCE

I have a small magnolia in a pot. When I glance out my office window and see the shiny green leaves, it always brings a smile. My magnolia has wrestled with the environmental conditions, like many people in Australia. During our catastrophic bushfire summer, it was smothered in ash and the buds stunted and fell off. Through months of heat and drought, the leaves burnt and shrivelled.

Following six months of intensive care – including liquid seaweed, mulching with sugar cane and supporting the soil with water-retaining crystals – new growth started to emerge from the dried sticks of its branches. One night it rained, and a tiny precious magnolia bud bloomed pure white, before it burned to a crisp with the strength of the afternoon sun. I celebrated this momentous milestone.

Bouncing back is what we do when we face disappointment, defeat and failure. Instead of wallowing or letting things keep us down, we get back up and continue with our lives.

Disappointment may look like missing out on a promotion or being passed up for an interesting project. Failure can be working really hard on an important presentation to the board that gets negative feedback. Defeat may look like bringing an important new product to market that dies through lack of sales and consumer interest.

Using a combination of mental adaptability and focusing our energy can help us minimise our emotional downtime and move faster towards recovery.

When we bounce forward, we learn from our adverse experiences and are stronger and better for them. We become better equipped to adapt and respond to life's pressures. While we might get knocked off course, we can move on from it.

Two helpful skill sets that support the bounce aspect of resilience are taking a growth mindset and optimism. Both are healthy mindsets that can be cultivated to give us options and pathways for when the going gets tough. Both help us to focus energy rather than leak energy when we need to marshal our resources.

Adopting a growth mindset

An open view enables us to learn more and view challenges and failures as opportunities to improve and grow.

With a fixed mindset, people believe their basic qualities, like intelligence or talent, are simply fixed traits. They believe that they are either smart or not, talented or not, and there is no way to change this. When people with fixed mindsets fail at something, as we all inevitably do, they tend to tell themselves that they can't or won't be able to do it. And they make excuses to rationalise the failure, like the proverb 'a poor workman blames his tools'.

Alternatively, with a growth mindset, people believe that their basic abilities can be developed through dedication and hard work. They believe that they can become smarter and better if they work hard and persevere. This view creates a love of learning and a resilience that is essential for progress and accomplishment.

After all, a poor workman who doesn't blame his tools can improve with practice and support.

Resilient people have more growth mindset characteristics. They don't wallow or dwell on failure; they acknowledge the situation, learn from their mistakes and then move forward.

Carol Dweck, a professor of psychology at Stanford University, has studied mindset for over 20 years. Her research shows that the view you adopt for yourself profoundly affects the way you lead your life. It can determine whether you become the person you want to be and whether you accomplish the goals you value.

Everyone has a mixture of fixed and growth mindsets, and that mixture continually evolves with experience. There are times when we believe in our talent and potential and see setbacks and failure as the process of getting better. Examples include the journey from beginner to proficient with a musical instrument, or committing to practise twice a week to improve our team's performance in a sporting competition.

At other times, we believe that our potential is limited by a lack of talent or our deficiencies. This could be when we decide we are 'hopeless' at drawing so don't even try. Or when the first cake we ever baked turned out like a pancake, and from then on, we became a 'bad cook'. When we adopt a fixed view, we give up at the first obstacle and let failure define us.

The passion for stretching yourself and sticking with something, even when it's not going well, is the hallmark of the growth mindset.

Growing a growth mindset

So, there is significant benefit in adopting a growth mindset. However, flexible thinking – or being able to 'go with the flow' – is much easier said than done, especially for those who tend to 'get stuck' in certain beliefs, thoughts and behaviour patterns.

You may have heard the expression 'black-and-white thinking'. This is where people have a fixed view of a situation, event, process or way of doing things. When we are stuck in this type of thinking, words like 'never' and 'always' are common. This may show up in self-talk like, 'There is no point in me trying to work out that maths problem, because I never get equations right,' or, 'Whenever I play netball, I always get injured, so I am better off not playing at all.'

Our brain remembers what we reinforce in our neural pathways, so if we're using the same 'facts' or telling the same stories all the time, we're stamping our neural pathways with them. This reduces our mental flexibility for certain situations and tasks, and we can struggle to accept new ideas and adopt different ways of doing things.

Our ability to cope with challenge and adversity can be influenced by how flexibly we are able to take alternative perspectives and interpret the situation we are in or what has happened to us. For example, finding a way to put it in perspective – such as thinking of those in worse situations – can be helpful, as can identifying some benefit that has come as a result of the difficulty experienced.

This isn't about denial of what happened or putting an unrealistically positive spin on things. But trying to find some good in negative events can be a healthy coping strategy.

Now it is your turn. What is your balance between fixed and growth mindsets?

What are your fixed mindset triggers? Examples could include receiving criticism, being compared poorly to others, earlier failures that undermined your confidence, or a workplace culture of blame.

In what aspects of your life do you adopt a growth mindset? How could you leverage this to benefit more areas of your life?

What strategies might you adopt to recognise when you start feeling threatened or defensive, to keep you in a growth mindset? For example, you could ask questions to understand more, ask for suggestions for improvement, ask for help, or create space to calm down before responding.

QUICK BITE

To develop your growth mindset, it is important to reward effort, learning and progress.

It is also important to acknowledge and encourage learning, such as by trying out new strategies, seeking help from others, experimenting and actively reflecting on new experiences.

Choosing optimism

Optimism is a mindset choice to view the world, other people and events in the most favourable, positive light possible. Think 'glass half full' rather than 'glass half empty'.

This helps you to bounce back and recover quicker from tough situations, and see options for bouncing forwards. Optimism doesn't mean glossing over or ignoring negative events or tough times, but rather recognising that challenges are temporary and expecting positive events in the future.

When the going gets tough, believe in your ability to handle it.

Resilient people see the positives in most situations and believe in their strength. They have a hopeful anticipation that future events will be favourable. This helps them handle problems from an empowered view with options, rather than adopting a victim mentality. There is a great saying that summarises this: 'When life hands you lemons, make lemonade.'

Science also shows that those with an optimistic outlook tend to be more proactive when it comes to their health, have better cardiovascular health and a stronger immune system – optimising energy.

Research shows that optimists are more likely to cope better and seek support from others, and less likely to withdraw from those around them. Through facing their issues and seeking advice, it is easier for them to see things more clearly and rationally; they can therefore be more realistic than pessimists.

To build optimism, focus on what you can do when faced with a challenge, and identify positive, problem-solving steps that you can take. This includes contingency planning and allowing for worst-case scenarios, but not burning emotional energy on the uncontrollables.

By directly tackling difficulties, and actively looking for benefits and learning in challenging situations, you will experience fewer negative emotions and less stress.

Now it is your turn. What is your relationship with optimism?

Optimism is 25% genetic and 75% shaped by our circumstances. What is your optimism starting point? Do you tend to come from a glass-half-full or glass-half-empty perspective?

When the going gets tough, what strategies work for you? What has helped you move through adversity and challenge in the past?

How can you incorporate more optimism into your daily life?

QUICK BITE

Here are my top tips for fostering optimism:

- Begin each morning by setting a positive intention.
- Hang out with optimistic, grounded friends and enjoy the halo of their positive energy.
- Limit your intake of the news, which can often be a barrage of negativity and a list of what is wrong in the world.
- Spend a few minutes each day journaling what you are grateful for.
- Face the negatives and take action in the areas of your life that are keeping you stuck.
- Recognise and invest in what you can control, and let go of worrying about what you can't control.

FINDING ZEST

Zest is about living life with a sense of excitement, anticipation and energy, and is an essential element that nurtures our soul, gives us spirit and makes us human. Those who have zest exude this energy in their approach to life, which can be truly contagious.

Zest means not approaching tasks or activities halfway or half-heartedly. People who are high in zest are excited to get up in the morning, and they live their lives like an adventure.

Building emotional agility and optimising energy provides a resilience springboard to create and live your best life with vitality and flow.

Zest makes a significant impact on the way we perceive failures, face adversities and bounce back onto the right track when we hit a bump in the road.

Zestful people are less neurotic and have better coping mechanisms than others. They are more likely to overcome failures and adversities with more efficacy than people who are less zestful.

Zest and happiness go together. Research shows that people with more zest are more satisfied with life. Zestful people also tend to be more satisfied with their jobs and are less prone to burnout and stress attacks.

Zest can take you further than you thought possible. Zest is your catapult.

Zestful people perform tasks wholeheartedly and focus more on the positive aspects of life. They are the people who will hold tight and not give up during times of distress. Zest is a positive trait that also includes ingredients of empathy, compassion, enthusiasm and ethics.

Developing zest

Feeling lively and high-spirited every day conditions our brain to form neural networks that make us feel joyful, which is why zestful people don't have to put in much effort to extract positivity – they reflect it spontaneously.

There are two key ingredients that support zest: purpose and flow. Both provide an emotional and energetic boost of ease rather than effort.

Knowing your purpose in life, connecting the activities that you do to something greater than the task and having a sense of meaning about how you show up in the world all boost zest. And those with a strong sense of purpose show better self-regulation and academic performance, and see the world as a more coherent place.

Flow is something we often experience in hobbies, such as music or sport – where we become so absorbed that we lose track of time. But creating engagement at work and experiencing a state of flow with our work is also a wellbeing boost.

This includes:

- being able to utilise our skills and abilities to the fullest – being fully absorbed or in flow with our activities on a regular basis
- aligning our values and belief systems to our actions, so that we derive maximum pleasure and satisfaction from everything we do
- developing secure and long-lasting interpersonal connections and relationships – both personally and professionally.

Now it is your turn. How is your zest? Are you boosting or draining your zest?

What are the activities that you engage in where you experience a sense of flow?

How do you keep track of the little moments of joy in your daily life?

How can you bring more zest into your day?

QUICK BITE

Here are some tips for boosting your zest:

- **Take care of your body:** Eat well, get enough sleep and move regularly. Exercise can make you more zestful if it's fun – try skipping the treadmill and joining a dance class.
- **Practise savouring:** Zest involves feeling fully engaged in the world with all your senses alive. You can build that feeling by slowing down and truly savouring positive events and sensory experiences – don't let them breeze past you without taking the time to fully enjoy them.
- **Revive a hobby:** Make time for hobbies where you lose yourself in time and smile. Think creative types of pursuits, such as music, crafting or gardening – hobbies where you create something, not passive activities such as binge-watching TV or going shopping.
- **Cultivate your optimism:** Feeling hopeful can boost your excitement and joie de vivre.
- **Get social:** Nurturing social connections, spending time with close friends, cultivating your relationships at work and participating in group activities all boost zest. Load up on oxytocin by sharing with friends and family what each of you are grateful for.
- **Experience nature:** Being around vibrant greenery can make you feel more zestful. Just a 15 minute walk outdoors increases your sense of vitality and energy, which is not experienced when walking indoors on a treadmill.

RESILIENCE RECIPE #6

FULL STEAM AHEAD

Christine turned up to my mentoring program in pretty bad shape. The accounts processing team and supervisor role that she had poured her heart and soul into for eight years was being made redundant and the work centralised into the head office in another city. To receive her redundancy payment, she needed to work right through to the handover date. Since the initial announcement, she had been in limbo for six months waiting for a handover date to be announced.

Emotionally, she was in a dark place and feeling drained. Mentally, she couldn't see a pathway forward with this organisation. And she was terrified at the prospect of having to start her career all over again somewhere else. She didn't hold much hope that the mentoring would help or that she would be around for the full program, but she needed something to brighten the monotonous uncertainty of her working days.

We started by looking at what was working well for Christine and within her control at work. She had a reputation as a good performer with a strong work ethic and had an enviable network of senior relationships across the organisation. So, we got her to call members of her network, share her current circumstances and ask about opportunities in other work areas.

Christine came to the next session brimming with opportunities and interviews for roles that she hadn't realised were possible. From one of those interviews, she was immediately offered a role. It wasn't a suitable role, but it reaffirmed her capability and boosted her confidence.

At the same time, Christine was looking for projects in other areas where she could continue to grow her experiences, skills and networks to make the most out of her time while waiting for her final date to be announced.

As Christine experimented with new tasks and challenges, she realised that she had a strong skill set that was transferable across several roles. She became increasingly sought out for her knowledge, enthusiasm and willingness to help others.

I also encouraged her to scope out her dream job. She told me that what she would really love would be a training role for process improvement of client services, but it didn't exist. As Christine applied for jobs, she was able to clearly articulate what her strengths were and also shared aspects of her dream job.

Nine months after we started working together, Christine's dream training role supporting a national business improvement project was created specifically for her. It was a 12-month contract, which previously she would have knocked back through lack of certainty. She came dancing through the door ecstatic and brimming with optimism over the possibilities of where this could lead her.

Flex, bounce and zest are springboards for optimising your engagement with life. Are you making the most of these wellbeing boosters?

CONCLUSION

SET YOURSELF UP FOR SUCCESS

Just as wellbeing and resilience are individual and unique to each one of us, what resonates and appeals to each of us will also be different. So, I invite you to cherrypick the resilience strategies that you will enjoy and start there.

No matter what strategies you choose, however, I recommend the following tips:

- Stick your definition of wellbeing somewhere visible where you will see it every day, such as above your desk, on the fridge or by your bed.
- Change starts with one tiny step forward. What is the smallest, easiest wellbeing-boosting activity that you can begin with? Set your day up for success by starting with wellbeing.
- Hold yourself accountable. Tell your family, friends, work colleagues and neighbours, and enlist their help in keeping you on track. Post your declaration and progress on how

you are going in the Resilience Recipes Facebook community and increase your cheer squad.

- Plan. By making an action plan, you are planning to succeed. A failure to plan is a plan to fail. Get yourself a pretty notebook and sparkly pen, use notes on your phone or download a planning app, and get real about taking action. Head over to resiliencerecipes.com, where you can download your copy of the guided exercises in this book in a consolidated coaching plan template.
- Need further motivation? Find a wellbeing buddy to share with, cheer on and support each other's progress. Receive a regular wellbeing boost by joining our Resilience Recipes Club for tips, inspiration, podcasts, videos, mindfulness moments, competitions, community support and events.

Choose to take back your control, prioritise self-care, plug the energy drains and boost the spring in your step with resilience.

This book isn't about reading it, knowing it and doing… nothing.

Let's go!

CONNECT WITH ME

Thank you for reading *Resilience Recipes*. My hope in writing this book is to support you to make space for wellbeing, and to cut through the wellness clutter with some quick and easy resilience boosters to help you get started.

My greatest joy would be to see your copy of this book full of scribbles, coloured highlights, Post-it Notes and tags. If that's what your copy looks like, please share a picture of it in the Resilience Recipes Facebook group, to help others take a step forward and unlock some bonus gifts for yourself.

If you want to keep your book in pristine condition, don't let that deter you from taking action. Head over to resiliencerecipes.com, where will find a coaching plan and loads of free templates, tips and other tools to support you.

I am super fortunate to do work I love with leaders and teams to leverage resilience and wellbeing as a performance advantage. To put it simply, the research now clearly shows that organisations that are well do well.

So, if you think you or your team could benefit from a resilience recipe to get things moving along, get in touch for a plan of action.

My daily wellbeing fix is yoga. Yoga provides me with the breathing discipline to create space for emotional and mental wellbeing. And I love the cumulative benefits of regular practice with better flexibility and strength for my body, mind and soul. I also prioritise mini wellbeing booster retreats moving mind, body and soul in the fresh mountain air or immersion by the sea.

If you would like to join one of my resilience retreats with a group of like-minded humans, drop me a note to learn more.

Be well!

Fleur

LET'S KEEP THIS CONVERSATION GOING!

Fleur Heazlewood
Fleur Heazlewood
Resilience Recipes
hello@blueberryinstitute.com
resiliencerecipes.com
blueberryinstitute.com

REFERENCES AND RESOURCES

INTRODUCTION

World Health Organization (WHO), *Mental well-being: resources for the public*, WHO, viewed 28 September 2021, <who.int/news-room/feature-stories/mental-well-being-resources-for-the-public>.

CHAPTER 1: THE WELLBEING WORRY

Aked, J. & Thompson, S., *Five Ways to Wellbeing*, the new economics foundation (nef), N.D., <neweconomics.org/uploads/files/d80eba95560c09605d_uzm6b1n6a.pdf>.

Michaelson, J., Mahony, S. & Schifferes, J., *Measuring Well-being: A guide for practitioners*, nef, N.D., <b.3cdn.net/nefoundation/8d92cf44e70b3d16e6_rgm6bpd3i.pdf>.

Oades, Dr L. & Heazlewood, F., *Wellbeing language & definitions guide*, Mental Health Commission of New South Wales, June 2017, <nswmentalhealthcommission.com.au/sites/default/files/inline-files/language-and-definitions-guide-web_0.pdf>.

Wheel of Well-being, viewed 28 September 2021, <wheelofwellbeing.org/about>.

CHAPTER 2: RESILIENCE TO THE RESCUE

McGonigal,K., *How to make stress your friend*, TEDGlobal, June 2013, <ted.com/talks/kelly_mcgonigal_how_to_make_stress_your_friend?language=en>.

Robertson Cooper, 'Resources', viewed 28 September 2021, <robertsoncooper.com/resources/>.

Windle, G., 'What is resilience? A review and concept analysis', *Reviews in Clinical Gerontology*, vol. 21, no. 2, 2011, pp. 152–169, <researchgate.net/publication/231842385_What_is_resilience_A_review_and_concept_analysis>.

CHAPTER 3: EMOTIONAL AGILITY

Achor, S., *The Happiness Advantage: The seven principles of positive psychology that fuel success and performance at work*, 2010.

Achor, S., *The happy secret to better work*, TEDxBloomington, May 2011, <ted.com/talks/shawn_achor_the_happy_secret_to_better_work?language=en>.

David, Dr S., *Emotional Agility: Get unstuck, embrace change and thrive in work and life*, Penguin Life, London, 2016.

David, Dr S., *The gift and power of emotional courage*, TEDWomen, November 2017, <ted.com/talks/susan_david_the_gift_and_power_of_emotional_courage?language=en>.

Fredrickson, B.L., 'History of Happiness: Barbara Fredrickson', Pursuit of Happiness, viewed 28 September 2021, <pursuit-of-happiness.org/history-of-happiness/barb-fredrickson/>.

Fredrickson, B.L., 'The emerging science of positive psychology is coming to understand why it's good to feel good', *American Scientist*, vol. 91, July–August 2003, pp. 330–335, <peplab.web.unc.edu/wp-content/uploads/sites/18901/2018/11/fredrickson2003amsci_english.pdf>.

Fredrickson, B.L., 'The Role of Positive Emotions in Positive Psychology: The Broaden-and-Build Theory of Positive Emotions', *American Psychologist*, vol. 56, no. 3, 2001, pp. 218–226, <peplab.web.unc.edu/wp-content/uploads/sites/18901/2018/11/fredricksonampsyc2001.pdf>.

Fredrickson, B.L., 'What Good Are Positive Emotions?', *Review of General Psychology*, vol. 2, no. 3, 1998, pp. 300–319, <peplab.web.unc.edu/wp-content/uploads/sites/18901/2018/11/fredrickson1998.pdf>.

CHAPTER 4: MENTAL ADAPTABILITY

American Psychological Association, 'Mindfulness meditation: A research-proven way to reduce stress', APA, 30 October 2019, <apa.org/topics/mindfulness/meditation>.

Brown, Dr B., 'Integration Idea: Empathy', Daring Classrooms, 2020, <https://brenebrown.com/wp-content/uploads/2020/01/Integration-Ideas_Empathy-2020.pdf>.

Goleman, D. & Davidson, R.J., *Altered traits: Science reveals how meditation changes your mind, brain, and body*, Avery, New York, 2017.

Hanh, Thich Nhat, *No Mud, No Lotus: The art of transforming suffering*, Parallax Press, Berkeley, 2014.

Hanh, Thich Nhat, *The Art of Living*, Ebury, London, 2017.

Hanh, Thich Nhat, *The Miracle of Mindfulness: A manual on meditation*, Beacon Press, Boston, 1987.

Hanson, Dr R., *Hardwiring Happiness: The new brain science of contentment, calm, and confidence*, Harmony Books, New York, 2013.

Hanson, Dr R. & Hanson, F., *Resilient: How to grow an unshakable core of calm, strength, and happiness*, Harmony Books, New York, 2018.

Hanson, Dr R. & Mendius, R., *Buddha's Brain: The practical neuroscience of happiness, love & wisdom*, New Harbinger, Oakland, 2009.

Headlee, C., *10 ways to have a better conversation*, TEDxCreativeCoast, May 2015, <ted.com/talks/celeste_headlee_10_ways_to_have_a_better_conversation?language=en>.

Mindfulness Meditation, viewed 28 September 2021, <mindfulnessmeditation.net.au>.

CHAPTER 5: OPTIMISING ENERGY

Baumeister, R.F. & Tierney, J., *Willpower: Rediscovering the greatest human strength*, Penguin, New York, 2012.

Clear, J., *Atomic Habits: Tiny changes, remarkable results: An easy and proven way to build good habits and break bad ones*, Avery, New York, 2018.

Huffington, A., *Thrive: The third metric to redefining success and creating a life of well-being, wisdom, and wonder*, Random House, New York, 2014.

Rath, T., *Eat Move Sleep: How small choices lead to big changes*, Missionday, 2013.

Sharma, R., *The 5 AM Club: Own your morning, elevate your life*, HarperCollins, Toronto, 2018.

Spall, B. & Xander, M., *My Morning Routine: How successful people start every day inspired*, Portfolio, 2018.

CHAPTER 6: FLEX, BOUNCE AND ZEST

Brach, Dr T., *Radical Acceptance: Embracing your life with the heart of a Buddha*, Bantam Books, New York, 2003.

Dweck, C., *Mindset: The new psychology of success*, Random House, New York, 2006.

Goleman, D., *Emotional Intelligence: Why it can matter more than IQ*, Bantam Books, New York, 1995.

Goleman, D., *Social Intelligence: The new science of human relationships*, Bantam Books, New York, 2006.

Houston, E., '10 Best TED Talks on VIA Character Strengths and Virtues', PositivePsychology.com, 17 November 2020, <positivepsychology.com/tedtalks-via-strengths-virtues/>.

Salzburg, S., *Lovingkindness: The revolutionary art of happiness*, Shambhala, Boston, 1995.

'Self Compassion', Centre for Clinical Interventions, Government of Western Australia, viewed 28 September 2021, <cci.health.wa.gov.au/Resources/Looking-After-Yourself/Self-Compassion>.

'Self-Compassion: Dr Kristen Neff', viewed 28 September 2021, <self-compassion.org>.

Seligman, M.E.P., *Flourish: A visionary new understanding of happiness and well-being*, Atria Paperback, New York, 2013.

Seligman, M.E.P., *Learned Optimism: How to change your mind and your life*, Pocket Books, New York, 1998.

NOTES